Grungewick

Introduction copyright © 2015 Michael Winkler
Copyright on individual newapper articles has expired, as per Australian Copyright Law.
This book is copyright. Apart from any fair dealing for the purpose of private study, research, criticism or review, as permitted under the Copyright Act, no part may be reproduced by any process without written permission.
The moral right of the author has been asserted.

Originally published as an ebook by Vivid Publishing 2015

Print edition: 2016
Cover design by Joe Winkler
Cover incorporates three copyright-free images from State Library of Victoria collection: Hoffman Brick & Potteries Limited, Brunswick [photo]; Brunswick Park Estate 1888 [cartographic material]; Melbourne and Metropolitan Board of Works Town of Brunswick Detail Plan No. 1896 [cartographic material].

National Library of Australia CIP Data
Title: Grungewick : gritty and gruesome news stories of early Brunswick / Michael Winkler (editor).

Subjects: Crime--Victoria--Brunswick--19th century.
 Brunswick (Vic.)--History.

Dewey Number: 364.1099451

Print ISBN: 978-0-9945798-1-2

Westbourne Books
www.michaelwinkler.com.au

Grungewick

Gritty and gruesome news stories of early Brunswick

Edited and introduced by
Michael Winkler

Introduction

I have lived more than half of my life in Brunswick. In 1987 I rented a one-bedroom flat in Glenlyon Road, bought some five-buck furniture from Vinnies in Albert Street, and started whinging about the tardiness of the number nineteen tram. Since that time I've lived in Luscombe, Victoria, Westbourne and Hope Streets; moved between the 3055, 3056 and 3057 postcodes; married my sweetheart in Brunswick Town Hall; and been bombed by at least two generations of teenagers down the deep end at the Baths.

My Dad boarded in a converted fernery in Eveline Street in the 1950s, and I like the way that extends my connection to the place, but I make no special claim to Brunswick authenticity. I felt like a local as soon as I moved in; I like to think that others do, too. Longevity doesn't necessarily mean loyalty. There's room for ownership by all.

Or at least there is now. Whether the people who first lived on this land regarded their relationship to country as ownership or guardianship, there was scant consideration of this connection when the land on which Brunswick stands transitioned from Indigenous to European control in the mid-1800s. I was astonished when researching this book at the almost complete non-appearance of Indigenous people in local nineteenth century newspapers. For tens of thousands of years the Wurundjeri people of the Kulin Nation lived, danced, hunted, fought, laughed, loved and died on the fertile plains between the Merri and Moonee Ponds Creeks, but within a few decades they were unworthy of mention in the press. Perhaps this was a deliberate erasure: the only thing more definitive than taking someone's territory is wiping them from the narrative. Alternatively, it might reflect the staggering decline in population due to active and passive methods of removal, including murder, disease and the seizure of land.

We are still living on their country. Sometimes I try to think what it might have been like here 200 or 2,000 or 20,000 years ago. Such a brief period of European intervention has resulted in the expunction of so much lore and learning. It is remarkable that most non-Indigenous people seem to have no conception or concern about how much we have all lost. Future generations might, but that is no consolation.

Beyond that seismic upheaval of European settlement, the next most dramatic change to the nature of Brunswick occurred during the past quarter-century. This is something I have been around to witness: the metamorphosis from a working-class to a middle-class suburb.

When I moved to Brunswick in 1987, Anglo-Australians were a minority. The textiles, footwear and clothing industries were still viable, and small factories proliferated, making everything from rope to socks – or, in the case of O. Kronos of Sydney Road, huge scarlet glory boxes strapped with brass. Families tended to be large, incomes were small, and the Bohemian element had minimal presence. Lots of warehouses; no 'warehouse conversions'. The only coffee shops were barren rooms frequented by men only, fogged with cigarette smoke and forbidding to outsiders. If I wanted a cappuccino I bought it from a greasy place in Barkly Square. The pubs were occasionally rough and generally depressing, including the Sporting Club Hotel where the topless bar staff startled takeaway shoppers by helping out in the bottle shop. On Sundays the streets were quiet, shops and libraries were shut, and trains did not run on the Upfield line.

Things changed, first slowly, then fast. The Brunswick Music Festival began in 1989. A few cafés emerged on Lygon Street that catered for the mainstream, including one run by wrestling legend Mario Milano. Paula opened her now-famous gelati shop one block from our house, near Tony's Fasta Pasta (which did not lasta). The Italian people who owned the house next door to us sold it to a poet, and a teacher of clowning moved in a few doors down. Still no money in the joint, still a suburb of concrete back yards and front gardens full of tomatoes and beans and zucchinis, but the mix was changing. This was the early 1990s.

A decade later, when my elder son started primary school, he was one of only two Anglo-Aussies in his Prep class. His school had 115 students but taught four languages – Italian, Greek, Turkish and Arabic – because the representation from each community was so strong. Nowadays the same school has four times as many children and only teaches one Language Other Than English. There is plenty of blond hair in the playground, and the kids' parents are as likely to be lawyers and academics as labourers or factory hands.

Brunswick today is replete with people like me – middle-class whites with small families, a belief in the verities of composting and public transport, a strange obsession with coffee and micro-brewed beer, eager to live in a suburb with a lively arts scene but unwilling to be kept awake at night by loud music. We complain about rates, worry about contaminated soil, drive Subarus and demand better bike lanes, try to get the mortgage paid off more quickly while still planning an overseas holiday, and wonder if there is a carbon-neutral way to tweet about the lack of heritage-wire fences on dual-occupancy developments.

I care about Brunswick. I'm here for the long haul. More of my friends live in this suburb than anywhere else. But I liked it more in my earlier days, when it was quirkier, daggier, and had not been homogenised by the great influx of People Like Me.

While the suburb has changed, one of its less charming attributes has not. It remains a place of violent deeds and sudden deaths. As I walk the streets I am aware of passing the pub where two gangsters were murdered, or the supermarket where an armed robber gunned down a security guard, or the piece of bike path where a commuter had her throat slashed one morning, or the boarding house that was burned out, or the 'chop shop' where two young men died in a shoot-out. I remember the exact place in the car park at Barkly Square – when Gangemi's fruit and veg shop still opened to the outside – where I saw a dead man spreadeagled one Saturday morning. Architecture changes; memories remain.

I am intrigued by that duality – that the place I call my home, where the people I love the most live, has a dark underside. It turns out that it was ever thus. I started reading newspaper stories about Brunswick in the nineteenth century, and discovered that this was never a place free of trouble.

I was in my late teens when I first encountered Michael Lesy's 1973 book *Wisconsin Death Trip*. I remember the sensation of flicking slowly through the pages of Charles Van Schaick's photographs: the sombreness they engendered, the head-shaking sense of hopelessness. That book includes some newspaper reports, and most of them feature death, disease and grinding poverty. The book was – is – entrancing and sombre. It allows someone divorced from that place by both time and space an inkling of what those experiences may have been like.

I have similar hopes for *Grungewick*. The newspaper reports reproduced here detail the bleaker aspects of nineteenth century life. It is not a balanced representation of Brunswick's portrayal in local newspapers of that time, let alone a fair picture of life in the suburb beyond the areas of newspaper interest – but it is not intended to be. A more rounded portrait would have included reports on football and cricket matches, calm and dull church meetings, public concerts, council discussions about drainage and development, a competitive ploughing event in Glenlyon Road. It would have reflected the proportion of newsprint given over to land sales, patent medicines, news from Europe, unvarnished verse, sentimental and possibly apocryphal stories allegedly from international sources, political grandstanding, horse racing, mild jokes.

No: this book is slanted. Some people lived comfortably and without incident in Brunswick of the 1800s, but they are not here. This book is about the other side of life – the melancholy, mendacious and even murderous side – and there is no lack of material. For some, life was proverbially nasty, brutish and short. There was a propensity to settle arguments with fists (or boots, or pieces of wood). Plenty of booze was consumed. Children were less likely to reach adulthood than they are now, and there was a greater risk of early death among adults.

I have included a number of articles about suicide and attempted suicide, because it was a major issue then as it is now. I am aware that current best practice for the news media is to avoid reporting suicide wherever possible. Nothing in this book glamorises the processes used, or glorifies the individuals involved. I have included these stories because they are among the most plangent, provide insights into a time when mental illness was stigmatised or misunderstood, and capture a very different journalistic approach than we see now. However, readers are obviously urged to exercise their own discretion with this material.

It is not only the stories about suicide that have the power to bruise. I transcribed some articles with glumness, others with shock. Transcribing reports on the death of little children is dreadful. Why, then, focus on the morbid rather than the uplifting? Because it is a distillation of one aspect of our history, and it helps stave off the forgetting. It is a corrective to those who think violence and crime are modern phenomena. It is also a way of paying small tribute to those whose names have been erased by time. When next you walk past the eastern end of the all-weather soccer pitch in Clifton Park, reflect for a moment that this is where three girls drowned in a water-filled hole. As you meander up Sydney Road, know that you are pushing past the ghosts of troublemakers who made the street corners their own. Next time you sigh about nanny-state OH & S regulations, spare a thought for the workers who suffered appalling injuries or were killed on old Brunswick work sites. As you purchase contraceptives, consider a time when infanticide was far more common, and unaffordable babies were placed with 'baby farmers'.

What was Brunswick like pre-Federation? Some of the buildings from that time are still standing, but many were shoddy and the majority have disappeared. There were open paddocks in West Brunswick, and the landscape was pock-marked with holes from quarrying and clay removal. The suburb was pungent from alleys lined with outdoor lavatories and their leaky pans, the Union Street slaughterhouse, filthy in-fill dumped into mined-out quarry sites, stagnant water in clay-holes, the animal aroma of goats, cattle and poultry, and horse manure on every road.

Social mores were different. Most people attended church, and many felt the Sabbath should be kept holy. Swearing was bad form. Employees were expected to work long hours. The big men of the area – always, of course, men – owned the land, sat on the Council and also meted out punishments to fellow citizens at the local court. A certain level of domestic abuse against women was accepted. Children were thrashed as common practice, both at home and at school. Formal education did not last long, with youngsters entering the workforce around the time they entered their teens, or even earlier.

An 1896 letter to the editor of *The Coburg Leader* described Brunswick as known for "bricks and pottery, mud and poverty". An economy based on bluestone and clay made it a tough place to live and work. Things were even harder when the 1890s depression removed work from the equation. Money was scarce, and employment – if you had it – was generally hard. If you were sick, or injured, or your house burned down, or your spouse died, that was lamentable but not unexpected. Industrial safety standards were dire, but low-paid workers were supposed to endure privations and take risks without complaint. Individual health was also approached differently, with patent medicines proliferating, doctors making expensive house calls, and mental health approaches ranging from the uninformed to the punitive. Smoking was sociable: in 1899 the Australian Natives Association held a smoke night at the Mechanics Institute which chuffed through 5,000 gaspers from the Cameo Cigarette Co.

In many ways, Brunswick then is completely different to Brunswick now. Some of the difficulties of that time came from being an 'outlying' suburb, including the high cost of transport, and the lack of a telegraph connection to the central fire station. On the other hand, there are resonant themes: the Council battling over the cost of keeping the Baths open; articulate advocates putting their cases for and against child immunisation; hoon driving (albeit on horseback or horse and cart); older people despairing of louche youths; endless bureaucratic pettifogging, including countless citizens charged by the court for such crimes as failure to have their name on their dray, wandering cattle, and defective closets; overt racism towards despised new arrivals, in this case the Chinese; and bad faith being shown towards adherents to other religions. Any of that seem familiar?

Unlike Lesy's book, there are no photographs in *Grungewick*. I adore old pictures, but my perception of the past is forever infused with sepia. Time spent looking at monochrome photographs means I cannot quite believe that Sydney Road had shops with red livery, carts painted green, men in blue shirts, women with coloured flowers in their hats. I cannot believe that anyone at that time – human or horse – ran fluidly and not with the jerky motion of early newsreels. My vision of the past has long been mediated through film and photos. Counterintuitively, reading though the agglomeration of newspaper articles provided me with a more vivid visual sense of that time than looking at old images.

The biggest motivation for producing this book was my desire to share the experience of reading scrappy news items that somehow have a compression and open-endedness reminiscent of Chekhov's stories. They go so far and no further, and inevitably provoke endless questions. Who were these people? Why did they do the things they did? What happened next? Sometimes there are answers, but often there are not, and the tales float away like phantasms.

Against this, there was one powerful reason not to make this book. In early 2012 an appalling rape and murder occurred just off Hope Street which devastated locals to an unprecedented degree. The horrific crime committed against Jill Meagher was also a crime against the people of her suburb. This outrage, which continues to affect so many people in Brunswick and beyond, made me think very carefully about why I was compiling *Grungewick*, especially when reproducing accounts of women being accosted on the street in the nineteenth century. I decided to continue with this book because it is important to see events in historical context, and to realise – troublingly, shamefully – that what happened to Ms Meagher was a particularly terrible incident on a continuum, not a once-off. It should not be forgotten that women in this suburb have been abused for a long time. While I am comfortable that there is an ethical justification for *Grungewick*, I sincerely hope this collection does not upset anyone still haunted by that obscene crime – or, indeed, any other.

Finally, I offer my respects to the unbylined journalists of the years 1849-99 whose work is gathered here. With their diligence, occasional flair, unexpected editorialising, love of commas and hatred of paragraphing, they have fixed the dramas of Brunswick in that era to the page, and helped prevent that part of our past being forgotten. I have maintained the original wording and punctuation of all articles, with the only alteration being the removal of the most obvious typos and the insertion of paragraphing in a few stories to aid intelligibility.

Michael Winkler
Brunswick

DOMESTIC INTELLIGENCE: THE BRUNSWICK ROBBERY

Two men, named Collins and Dignam, who had been arrested upon suspicion of robbing Messrs. Morris and Meyers, last week, at Brunswick, were brought before the police bench on Friday last. In consequence of the non-attendance of Sergeant O'Neil, of the Mounted Police, who arrested the prisoners, and the absence of any evidence to connect them with the offence, they were discharged. Councillor Condell, who presided, animadverted in strong terms upon the conduct of Sergeant O'Neil in neglecting to attend the police office, and expressed a hope that Capt. Mair would take notice of the proceeding.

(The Argus, 23 January 1849)

DOMESTIC INTELLIGENCE: HIGHWAY ROBBERY

On Thursday evening last, as Mr. and Mrs. Lyall were returning from the Races to their residence on the Merri Creek, they were attacked by two armed men near the "Retreat Inn", at Brunswick, who robbed them of about £3 and then decamped. This is the third robbery perpetrated in the same neighbourhood within the past six months.

(The Argus, 3 April 1849)

DARING OUTRAGE

On Saturday night a poor widow, named Hennessy, residing at Brunswick, was waylaid a little beyond the Gaol, while on her road home, by three men, who, after knocking her down, robbed her of 1s 6d in cash and a few groceries which she had purchased for the forthcoming week. Mrs. Hennessy observed the men watching her during the early part of the evening while purchasing the above articles, and would be able to identify them if apprehended.

(The Argus, 5 June 1849)

BRUNSWICK

John Emmett, a man dressed in the garb of a digger, was charged with making an attempt on his own life. Mr. Clinton, the landlord of the Brunswick Hotel, Brunswick, stated that he saw the prisoner in an outhouse of his hotel on the previous day with his throat cut, and under such circumstances he had no doubt but that the injury had been inflicted by himself. The wounds did not appear to be so serious as to endanger life. The Bench remanded the prisoner for seven days for medical inquiry.

(The Argus, 4 March 1858)

BRUNSWICK

William H. Earl was charged with assaulting his wife. Mrs. Earl was sworn, but said she forgave her husband, and declined to say anything against him.

John Rollo, of Brunswick, was sworn, and said: I saw the prisoner last night in a tent at Brunswick. I heard a scuffle when I was at a distance, and cries of "Murder!" I looked in at the door, and saw the prisoner holding down a female. I called out to him, and he came out, followed by the woman. The woman said the prisoner was trying to strangle her, and that he had threatened to kill her several times. I gave the man in custody, and the woman laid the information against him.

The prisoner stated that his wife had attempted to throw a kettle of boiling water over him, and that he was only trying to tie her hands behind her when Mr. Rollo called out to him.

Mrs. Earl said that all she wanted was for the prisoner to be bound over to keep the peace. She was very aggravating in her temper – perhaps worse than he was. She thought they had better both of them be bound over to keep the peace.

The Bench dismissed the case, recommending both parties to make an effort to keep the peace without being bound over.

Maria Baily was charged with being drunk and stealing a purse containing £17, and some other property, from the person of James Burns. The prosecutor said he was coming from Brunswick on an omnibus, the previous night, and the prisoner was sitting next to him. He fancied he felt her hand in his pocket, but was not sure. He subsequently missed the purse. The police said that every search had been made for the property in the haunts frequented by the woman, but that it could not be found. The prisoner was fined 10s. for drunkenness, or in default 24 hours' imprisonment, and the graver charge was dismissed.

(The Argus, 2 June 1858)

BRUNSWICK

Martha Bingham, on a charge of larceny, was sentenced to fourteen days' imprisonment. The evidence was perfectly clear as to her guilt, as, also that her position was attributable to the degrading influence of strong drinks...

Moritz Krause, a poor old German, was fined 1s., and 2s. 3d. costs, for an unstamped weight, with which he weighed grapes for disposal, the produce of his own little garden.

(The Argus, 12 April 1866)

INQUESTS

Mr. Candler held an inquest at the Hospital on Monday, on the body of the unfortunate man Mark Palmer, who died on Sunday from the effects of injuries received on Thursday morning by the fall of a quantity of clay in a clay-pit at a brickyard at Brunswick, where he was employed. The jury found that the accident was purely accidental.

(The Argus, 16 June 1868)

BRUNSWICK

A drunken fellow named Richard Dooley was charged with wilful exposure in a public place. The offence was proved, and he was sent to gaol for one month, with hard labour.

(The Argus, 8 October 1868)

SAD MACHINERY ACCIDENT

A sickening and fatal accident took place in Brunswick at the pipe manufactory of Mr Thomas Kelly, or Brunswick, about 4 p.m. on Saturday. One of Mr Kelly's sons, about nine years of age, while standing too near the powerful machinery, allowed some part of his clothing to come into contact with the cog-wheel, which slowly but surely dragged him to destruction. The engine was stopped instantly, but it was found that the whole of the flesh of one leg had been completely taken from the bone, besides lesser injuries to the hand.

A cab fortunately was soon obtained, which conveyed him full gallop to the Melbourne Hospital, where death soon put an end to his sufferings. It is a fact worthy of note that had not the engine been stopped so promptly, further injury to two other lads, who bravely attempted to extricate him, would have had to be recorded, but fortunately, merely their clothing was torn.

(The Ballarat Star, 27 July 1869)

INQUEST

The district coroner held an inquest at Brunswick, on Saturday, on the body of a child named Jacob Stanley, aged two years. The deceased was with an elder sister at the house of a stonemason, named Shackleton, about half-past 3 o'clock on Friday afternoon. When his sister was going away, she missed the deceased, who had been playing about the house, and, going outside to look for him, she

found him lying on the ground, with a large stone on him. She immediately lifted the stone off, and called for Mrs. Shackleton. Mr. Talbot was sent for, but the child was quite dead.
    The stone was intended for a window sill, and was placed on its edge, and supported by two pieces of wood. The deceased was not heard to cry out either by Mrs. Shackleton or his sister. The jury found that the deceased was accidentally killed by a stone window sill falling on him.
(The Argus, 20 September 1869)

BRUNSWICK
    Joseph Hilton was charged with exposing obscene pictures. The prosecution was at the instance of the police, and the pictures referred to consisted of valentines with a decidedly lewd tendency, which had been exposed in defendant's window for sale, for which offence he was ordered 24 hours' imprisonment, with 5s. 6 d. costs...
    John O'Keefe, found guilty of breaking a plum-tree, was fined 2s. 6d., with 2s. 6d. damages and 5s. costs, or 24 hours' imprisonment.
(The Argus, 9 February 1872)

TWO CHILDREN DROWNED AT BRUNSWICK
    On Friday afternoon, between 3 and 4 o'clock, several children had gone to play on the banks of the Merri Creek. Maggie Williams, a little girl of the company, was wheeling in a barrow Louis, a little fellow two years old, the son of a poor German named Carl Raitschel, living in Albion-street. The sister of Louis, named Louisa, and ten years old, was also of the company. By some mishap the barrow got upset, precipitating the little boy into the creek, which in that particular place, the bottom of Albion-street, is some 20 feet deep.
    Without a moment's hesitation the brave and loving

sister threw herself into the water to endeavour to save her sinking brother. The children on the bank saw the convulsive struggling of the boy and girl, as once and twice they arose to the surface, and ran screaming for assistance, but before help could be had the little innocent and his noble-hearted sister had sunk finally beneath the water...

After a long and painful search both bodies were recovered, and carried to their bereaved parents' house, about 600 yards from where the melancholy catastrophe took place. The event, with its melancholy surroundings, caused a deep sensation in the neighbourhood.

(The North Eastern Ensign, 17 December 1872)

BRUNSWICK COURT

James Hutton was charged with permitting a nuisance to exist in the vicinity of a closet on his premises. Mr. Ramsay appeared for the prosecutors, and Mr. Gillott for defendant. It appeared from the evidence that a constable visited the premises of defendant, and found the nuisance which was complained of. It was stated for the defence that instructions had been given to remove the nuisance but they had not been complied with previous to the visit of the policeman. Dr. Talbot deposed that he considered the condition of the premises injurious to health. After consultation for some time, the magistrates dismissed the charge without costs.

(North Melbourne Advertiser, 17 April 1874)

THE RESULT OF CARELESS DRIVING

Mr S. J. Wesson, a grocer living in Weston street, Brunswick, was sued in the County Court on Thursday, by Roger Flaherty, a carter, for £1,000 damages, caused through the negligent driving of the defendant's son, a boy 10 years old. Some time ago Flaherty was in Cameron street, Brunswick, driving a horse in a cart loaded with over two tons of stone, when the defendant's son came along the same street, and, as was alleged, through careless driving, ran the wheel of a spring cart he was driving against the plaintiff, and jammed him up between the spring-cart and his own cart, in consequence of which plaintiff's spine was injured, and he became unable to work. It was also considered that he would never be able to work again at the occupation he had followed.

His Honour Judge Cope, after hearing a good deal of evidence, said he considered that the accident arose from the incompetent driving of the defendant's son, and that the father was answerable for the conduct of the son, as he was going on business by his parent's orders. He therefore returned a verdict for plaintiff, damages £150.

(North Melbourne Advertiser, 3 July 1874)

BRUNSWICK COURT

Michael Gately, the common hangman, charged a boy named Healy with wilfully damaging property to the value of £2. On the 24th of last month Gately was selling oranges and lemons, and stated that the lad wilfully upset the basket off his head. Mrs. Price, who resides close to the toll gate where the alleged affair took place, gave evidence that the lad did not upset the basket, but on the contrary, that Gately was drunk and fell down with it, and also chased the boy with a knife, using most abusive and offensive language. The police also proved that he was locked up on the day in question for being drunk. The case was dismissed, costs being given against Gately for 28s.

(North Melbourne Advertiser, 10 July 1874)

SHOCKING ACCIDENTS

A series of accidents occurred in a couple of brick works in Brunswick recently. The first happened to a youth named Stewart, in the brickyard of Trenoveth Brothers, at

Brunswick. He incautiously looked over the hopper of the pug-mill when in full motion, and his head got jammed by the revolving beam, at the end of which a horse was attached. The animal was stopped instantly, but not before the lad's jaws were broken, and it is reported his skull also.

About the same time, at the works of the Hoffman's Brick Company, a labourer named Pettett by some means slipped from his work, falling over forty feet on to loosened earth, which broke the fall considerably. In his case the collar bone and several ribs were broken, and he was subsequently removed to the Melbourne Hospital in great agony.

(North Melbourne Advertiser, 11 December 1874)

AN ESCAPED LUNATIC

On Saturday Constable Burke arrested a man (supposed to be an escaped lunatic) on the Sydney road, Brunswick. He is a quiet looking fellow, and accosted the constable as "your Royal Highness" each time he asked him some frivolous question. From the conversation which ensued, the man was arrested as a lunatic, and from the brands on the inside of the coat and vest, there appears to be little doubt of his having escaped from some asylum. The vest has simply L arrow A on the breast, while the coat has, in addition, M.D. underneath. He tells the police he has "been living in the wilderness for 15 years on dead men's bones, till the ghosts frightened him away, and that an Irish ghost named O'Ferrall, whom he had known in the old country, had stolen his boots, and given him the old ones in exchange."

He was sent to the Yarra Bend yesterday, where he was well known for having been an inmate for twelve years. He had only been at large a day or two, and is regarded as a very harmless creature.

(North Melbourne Advertiser, 22 January 1875)

CASUALTIES

Thomas Barry, living at Brunswick, was admitted to the Melbourne Hospital on Wednesday, suffering from concussion of the brain and bruises on the head caused by a fall. He had a fit while standing upon a plank, repairing machinery at Hoffman's patent brick factory, Brunswick, and fell about 9ft. to the ground.

(North Melbourne Advertiser, 19 March 1875)

THE BRUNSWICK EXHIBITION

The Brunswick exhibition continues to attract numerous visitors, or rather it would be more correct to say the singing and music are the chief sources of interest. The millinery begins to look rather faded, Hoffman's bricks have lost their interest, Cornwall's pottery works are shorn of their novelty and the ingenious instrument devised to assist smokers no longer excites their admiration. If it was not for Mr Wilks and the organ this Brunswick young ladies' promenade would soon become a sort of deserted village.

(North Melbourne Advertiser, 21 May 1875)

A MAN AND BOY DROWNED AT BRUNSWICK

Considerable excitement was occasioned in Brunswick yesterday afternoon by a report that a man and a boy had been drowned in one of the quarry-holes in Park-street. A large crowd soon gathered on the spot, to find that the report was too true. It appears that a middle-aged man named James Yendall was married a second time, some two years since, to a Mrs. Smith, who had a son about nine years of age. Yesterday, at about dinner time, Yendall was going to punish the boy for some misconduct, when he ran off in the direction of the holes, pursued by his stepfather.

The lad entered one of these dangerous places, going into the water nearly to his arm pits, and refused to come out unless a promise were given that he should not be beaten.

Rather than submit, Yendall walked in also, and in the most extraordinary manner both disappeared simultaneously.

All efforts at assistance were unavailing, as those on the spot say neither the man nor the boy rose again to view. The police subsequently dragged the hole as well as they could with the primitive appliances at hand, and after two hours' work managed to land the body of the man, which was subsequently removed to the house, at the pressing request of deceased's wife, who was fearfully distressed. Darkness coming on, further search was abandoned until a boat could be obtained, or a raft constructed, which will enable a more systematic search to be made for the body of the boy.

Yendall is said to be a native of Sweden, has been for many years engaged in quarrying in Brunswick, and has enjoyed the respect of those who knew him as a quiet, steady, hard-working man,

(The Argus, 7 July 1875)

ROBBERY IN BRUNSWICK

An impudent robbery was committed on Tuesday evening, in Union-street, Brunswick. A man named John Luther, in the employ of Mr. Heller, at the slaughterhouse, who occupies a room attached to the stables, left the place for the purpose of getting his tea, in Mr. Heller's house, on the other side of the yard about half-past 5, and returned again in 20 minutes, when he found that the place had been entered, and his box carried away. The box contained, in addition to clothing, a Post-office Savings Bank passbook, and deeds of other property. As Luther is well known to be earning good wages, and a man of very frugal habits, it is surmised that the robbery was effected by some person familiar with the premises, and the habits of the loser.

(North Melbourne Advertiser, 9 July 1875)

UNRULY CONDUCT IN CHURCH

Sir –

Will you permit me, through your journal, to express my surprise, at a step taken on Sunday the 8th inst. at the Wesleyan Church, Brunswick. During service, a little boy was talking pretty free – rather too free from some in the church – when two gentlemen rose from their seats, took hold of the little fellow, and, without mercy, dragged him out of the church, and through so doing, caused such a disturbance, that a young fellow, who ought to have better sense, walked out also; and seeing the brother to the one that was dragged out, defending him, walked up to him, and with shut fists offered to fight him, even on the church steps.

Church stewards should try and do things calm, and not get in such a temper about nothing. If preachers would shorten their sermons, it would make things far different to what they are, and not weary the children. Just look at two or three young women in one of the cushioned seats in the church, young women whose ages vary from twenty to "thirty" years, daughters of a councillor or a preacher, who cannot find time to grin only when in church. If children see that, what better can we expect from them.

Trusting you will excuse me for the space I have taken, I remain, your's &c.,

S.W.B., Brunswick

(North Melbourne Advertiser, 20 August 1875)

DEATH OF MR. FARRAR, OF BRUNSWICK

Mr. Farrar, who had gained some notoriety as the persistent agitator for full weight bread in Melbourne and suburbs, better known in Brunswick as "Big Loaf", died recently at an advanced age, at his residence, Albert street, Brunswick. He was deservedly much respected by a large circle of friends.

(North Melbourne Advertiser, 3 March 1876)

LETTER TO THE EDITOR

Sir –

On Tuesday week a public meeting was held in the Primitive Methodist Chapel, Union Street, Brunswick, in connection with the Sunday School held in that place. Mr. Eckersall read the report in which he stated that the late teachers held a large amount of money, and had not left any financial statement when the meeting closed. As I had been treasurer of the late school, I wished to give an explanation, as the chairman declined to take any notice, I then got on a form and attempted to give the explanation myself, but someone started the harmonium. I waited as well as the congregation until they were done, then I commenced again, but no sooner did I begin than the music started again, then Mr. E. Martin, blacksmith, of Sydney road, pushed me violently off the form and offered to fight, the[n] Mr. Eckersall assisted to push me down the aisle of the chapel causing me to come in contact with the ends of the seats to the danger of my limbs. A friend coming to my assistance was set upon by the first named worthy.

The explanation I desired to make was the treasurer's book and vouchers were taken by the Rev. Joshua Smith, Superintendent of the Circuit, on the 6th day of October, 1874, and I hold the receipts for the same. I may also state that the Rev. J. Smith and another audited the books and found them correct. Now, Sir, why not leave me have my say, and if I was wrong, prove me so; this is the style in which things have been done in the Primitive Methodist Church for a long time, as many besides myself can testify, without fear of contradiction, and woe betide the person who dares oppose the clique.

I remain, &c.,
J. Perry, Brunswick
(North Melbourne Advertiser, 3 March 1876)

SUSPICIOUS DEATH AT BRUNSWICK

Mr. Candler held an inquest on the 14th and 15th inst., at Brunswick, on the body of Margaret Swords, aged eight weeks, child of Walter Swords, labourer. Dr. Talbot, who made a post-mortem examination, deposed that the child was greatly emaciated, but that there were no external marks of violence. The cause of death was congestion of the brain, from the low state of vitality of the child, not from suffocation or other abnormal cause. There was no evidence of gross neglect. Had attended the mother for diarrhoea, which might have weakened her milk. What the child wanted was a healthy wet-nurse. The suddenness of the death was accounted for by the congestion of the brain.

Mary Ann Timms, nurse, stated that the child was apparently healthy, and was suckled by the mother, who had a good supply of milk. When witness next saw the child, 10 days or a fortnight later, it was pining away. The mother's husband was very abusive to her.

Clara Miller, daughter of Mary Ann Swords by a former husband, stated that her mother drank a little at times since the birth of the child, but did not drink habitually. After the birth of the child Swords often struck and knocked down his wife, but never hurt the baby, though he struck her when she had the child in her arms. The man was in the habit of drinking, and used to beat witness, who the night before the child died went away at 11 o'clock to a neighbour's house for fear of him.

Mary Ann Miller, sister of the last witness, said that the husband kicked her mother in bed the night before the child died. About 6 o'clock in the morning witness went out for her sister, and when she came back found the child dead in her mother's arms. Dr. Talbot, recalled, said he was still of the same opinion as before about the child's death, but considered the condition of the mother might have been injuriously affected by the ill-treatment from her husband.

The jury found that the child died from congestion of the brain, from the low state of vitality, and that though the evidence was not sufficient to show that the child's death was accelerated by the conduct of Walter Swords in

ill-treating the mother, yet that it showed that he ill-treated her in a most brutal manner.
(The Argus, 17 March 1876)

WANDERING GOATS

A little before 2.30p.m. on Wednesday, 29th March, fronting the Brunswick Police Court, three goats were to be seen staring at, and cocking their tails, before two magistrates who had just retired from their duties. Just as the goats were performing these peculiar antics a storm coming on at that moment dispersed both goats and magistrates, and strange to say two of the goats alluded to belong to an employee of the Borough Council.
(North Melbourne Advertiser, 7 April 1876)

BRUNSWICK COURT

W. Buchanan was proceeded against by Sergeant O'Shaughnessy for attempting to commit suicide. He was discharged, as the witness who sold the poison to him had gone to Sandhurst, and cannot be found.
William Freer, a young man, was charged with the same offence as the above defendant. He tried to rid himself of his life by hanging by his neck to a clothes line in the yard, but he happened to be seen before he could accomplish his object. He was remanded for one week.
(North Melbourne Advertiser, 16 June 1876)

BRUNSWICK POLICE COURT

Mr. McCarter proceeded against Hannibal Mathews for discharging firearms within the borough without the permission of the local authorities and thereby killing two of his valuable geese. He was fined 5s. with 2s. 6d. costs.
Hannibal Mathews, the defendant in the above case,

proceeded against Mrs. McCarter, the plaintiff in the same case, for cruelly il[l]treating his dog by throwing a dip[p]er full of hot water over it. She was fined 5s. with 2s. 6d. costs.

(North Melbourne Advertiser, 14 July 1876)

BRUNSWICK CABS

A Brunswick correspondent writes of "the exorbitant charges, and the irregular times of running of these cabs; the Sydney road is the most expensive one for travellers of any round Melbourne. Men who work in Melbourne and are anxious for their families to reside in this healthful suburb cannot do so; 6d. for an ordinary fare, and 1s. if after seven o'clock, is what very few persons can afford. The charges are really extortionate. The roads are now in good order. Why is there not some movement to secure the busses on this road. It is the only one now without those cheap, comfortable, and well managed vehicles."

(North Melbourne Advertiser, 28 July 1876)

THE BRUNSWICK ROAD

Of all the inlets to Melbourne city there is none that should be more grand and attractive than the great Sydney-road; or, to use the name usually applied to it, the Brunswick.

But this fine highway labours under the serious disadvantage of being nearly always in an extremely bad state of repair. There is an immense traffic on it, chiefly of stone and brick laden drays, among which hay and corn laden carts make a not altogether inconsiderable show, and the traffic sustained by the road contributes to its maintenance by paying toll-gate fees. Still the roadway is in a wretched condition. Some months ago there was only one wheel-track on it, and this was so deeply rutted by the passing, citywards, of heavy loads, that the unfortunate animals engaged in drawing the drays in questions had two or three times their legitimate work to perform.

Later on, the road was repaired or re-made, and for a time the horses working upon it had something like fair play. But only for a very short time. Soon the metal put upon the road got ground into powder, to fly about on the wings of every wind that blew, and destroy the furniture and wall hangings of the villas and cottages that line the road on its western side, while the wheel ruts speedily reappeared, to the annoyance and distress of the animals condemned to travel the highway with collars about their necks...

(The Argus, 21 April 1877)

INQUEST

Dr. Youl held an inquest at the Melbourne Hospital on Thursday, on the body of Charles Edward Clark, aged 24 years, a newsagent, residing in Brunswick, who fell from a horse in Albert-street, Brunswick, on Wednesday, and who died soon after his admission to the hospital. James Giles, a brickmaker, said that he saw the accident. The deceased was delivering newspapers on horseback, and was riding at a slow gallop, when one of the stirrups broke, causing him to lose his balance, and he fell off on his head. Witness picked him up, and finding that he was quite insensible took him to a doctor, upon whose advice he was taken to the hospital. He died in the afternoon without regaining consciousness. The cause of death was compression of the brain and fracture of the base of the skull. The jury returned a verdict of accidentally killed.

(The Argus, 4 January 1878)

POLICE

At the Brunswick Court on Wednesday, the recent case arising from the greyhound nuisance was again heard. On this occasion H. Barningham charged William Anderson, the trainer for Mr. James, with "wilfully permitting dogs to worry a cat". According to plaintiff's version, the dogs, some of which were muzzled, rushed into his yard and seized a favourite cat, tearing it to pieces before rescue could be attempted, and one witness deposed to seeing Anderson's boy follow in and take the dying cat out of the mouth of one of the dogs. For the defence Anderson swore all his dogs were securely muzzled, but admitted that some strange dogs had joined his, and contended it was the strangers that had inflicted the injuries, which he was powerless to prevent. The Bench inflicted a fine of 10s., with 35s. costs.

(The Argus, 24 May 1878)

FIRE AT BRUNSWICK
A fire of considerable dimensions broke out in Brunswick about 2 o'clock yesterday morning, in a large wooden building used as a furniture factory by H. M. Smith, the proprietor. The fire was first discovered by Constable Murray, who lost no time in alarming Mr Smith and the neighbours, and then endeavoured to get the telegraph in motion for the Melbourne Fire Brigade, but it was found that through Brunswick being "cut out" at night, no message could be transmitted.

The burning building was situated at the rear of the business premises, and from the inflammable nature of the contents and the strong westerly wind blowing, a number of small cottages in the line of fire were in great danger for a considerable time from the falling sparks; but as a plentiful supply of water was at hand, the various owners and occupiers were enabled to prevent any damage being done. A small cottage on the windward side, some 40ft. distant, was very much scorched, and only saved by quantities of water being dashed on the walls.

The Melbourne Brigade were on the ground about 35 minutes after the break-out, but not being able to find a plug within a reasonable distance did not succeed in getting a jet. The Carlton Brewery Brigade arrived some five minutes after, and were more fortunate, for in a very short time some 400ft. of hose was run out, and a fine volume of water was got on to the burning mass.

Mr Smith is uninsured as far as the materials and tools are concerned, and estimates his loss at between £600 and £700. A policy of £100 is on the building, but as that is only to cover advances by a building society he will not participate in it. How the fire originated is a mystery, as the building was erected on red gum piles, some 9ft. high, and was only accessible by a flight of steps, and the door was still locked on the discovery of the outbreak. An inquest will probably be held.

(The Argus, 3 June 1876)

BRUNSWICK - Wednesday

A man named Hegarty was charged by the Inspector with furious driving, the Inspector's evidence being corroborated by the police. It transpired that this freak is a favourite pastime with Mr. Hegarty, who had to pay for this latest exploit 10s and 2s 6d costs, or three days' imprisonment.

(Mercury and Weekly Courier, 1 November 1879)

BRUNSWICK - Wednesday

Jas. Hegarty was charged with being drunk and disorderly on the evening of the 18th inst. He is in the habit of getting drunk about 104 times a year – that is about twice weekly – and is one of the greatest nuisances of the Borough of Brunswick, and gives more trouble to the police than any other resident of the district. Mr. Shuter pointed out to him the error of his ways in a lengthy speech, and fined him 10s, with 5s 6d costs.

(Mercury and Weekly Courier, 27 November 1880)

BRUNSWICK - Wednesday

William Ogilvie, of Barkley-street, Emily Watson of Weston-street, and F. Cosans, Sydney-road, were charged with selling bread without weighing it in the presence of the purchaser. Mr. Grylls appeared for the prosecution, and clearly proved the offence in each case. Mr. Leonard appeared for the defendant Cosans, and asked the Bench to deal lightly with his client, on the ground that purchasers of bread so frequently requested the seller not to mind weighing it, that they (the sellers) were apt to occasionally forget to do so. The loaf bought from Cosans was 2½ ozs. short of weight, and those from Watson's and Ogilvie's, 1¾ ozs. short each; but these facts were not brought out in the evidence. The Bench inflicted a fine of £1 and £1 5s costs in each case, or in default distress.

(Mercury and Weekly Courier, 11 February 1882)

BRUNSWICK - Wednesday

A Chinaman, named Long Fang, was charged with stealing water of the value of 5s, the property of the Board of Land and Works. It was clearly shown that the water-pipe had been disconnected from the meter, and the water thus used without passing through it. In the present instance the quantity stolen was estimated at about 5500 gallons. How often the water has been stolen in like manner it is impossible to say, but in all probability theft of this nature by Chinamen for watering their gardens "on the cheap" is of frequent occurrence.

Long Fang, through the interpreter, Mr. Hodges, endeavour[ed] to show that the pipe was disconnected purely by accident and that, previous to the visit from the Water Inspector a plumber had been applied to repair the damage, but that he had failed to do so until after the officer's visit. Long Fang also expressed a wish that in the event of his being found guilty their Worships would deal mercifully with him, as he was an old man and this was the first time he had been before a court of justice since he came to the colony.

Mr. Shuter, in sentencing the prisoner to one month's imprisonment with hard labor, remarked that thefts of this nature were frequently committed, but that few persons were convicted for the same on account of the extreme difficulty of detecting the frauds, and consequently when these thefts were discovered it behoved that they should be dealt with severely.

(Mercury and Weekly Courier, 11 March 1882)

INCENDIARISM AT BRUNSWICK

At the Brunswick Police Court on Wednesday last, Mary Ann Murphy, in conjunction with a man named McLeish, were charged with maliciously and wilfully setting fire to certain matter in immediate proximity to a building. From the evidence of Elizabeth Brown, a girl of respectable and prepossessing appearance, in the employ of Mr. A. Melville, of Brunswick-road, it appears that at about noon on Tuesday the 23rd ultimo, she (witness) seeing a quantity of smoke in the yard adjoining McLeish's property, went into the yard and looking over the fence saw the female prisoner come out of McLeish's kitchen with a shovel-full of live coals and burning wood, which she threw over the fence against the wall of Melville's house which is built of wood.

She then emptied the contents of a black bottle upon the embers and, McLeish coming out, asked him for a match, which he produced, and striking it, applied to the liquid which had been poured on the fire, by thrusting his arm through a gap in the fence. The fire immediately blazed up with great force, charring and disfiguring the side of Melville's house to a height of about six feet. At this point the girl ran into the house calling to Mrs. Melville that some one was setting fire to the house. On coming into the yard Mrs. Melville jumped upon a box by the side of a fence, and with a bucket of water which her niece handed to her, endeavoured to extinguish the fire.

Whilst doing so the female prisoner rushed at her

with a broom handle, with which she struck her across the head. Mrs. Melville then sent for the police, who arrested Murphy, and from information afterwards received, ultimately summoned McLeish for aiding and abetting. Mr. Grylls appeared for Murphy, who denied all connection with the fire, as did also the prisoner McLeish, endeavouring to cast the blame on her son, a boy of about six years of age, who she stated had been playing with matches and had set fire to an old shirt which was hanging upon the fence and this the prisoners alleged was the only thing burnt, they had flogged the boy for doing it.

Mrs. McLeish supported this view of the case, admitting, however, that both prisoners were under the influence of drink at the time, and that the fire had originated in her absence. On her return she had found both prisoners in the front room of her house just as she had left them about quarter of an hour previous, but on going to the back she saw a volume of smoke and giving the alarm she immediately poured two buckets of water upon the flame, which together with that thrown by Mrs. Melville had effectually extinguished the fire. On turning to the child who had stood on one side, she found some matches in his hand, and a box of same in his pocket.

The male prisoner stated that Mrs. Melville when putting out the fire, had used foul language to Murphy in consequence of which she (Murphy) had struck her with the broom handle. During the hearing of the evidence the female prisoner fainted, upon which the court adjourned for ten minutes. At the conclusion of the case Mr. Grylls said that he was at a loss to understand the matter. He would not for a moment hint that the witness Brown had wilfully committed perjury, for his part she had given her evidence in such a straightforward and unhesitating manner that he scarcely knew what to think, but yet he would draw the attention of the bench to the gravity of the charge, and he hoped they would duly weigh the contrary evidence before giving their decision.

After a short deliberation the prisoners were committed for trial, bail for Murphy being refused, as she

was considered to be a most dangerous character, whilst McLeish was allowed bail in two sureties of £50 each.
(Mercury and Weekly Courier, 3 June 1882)

BRUNSWICK - Wednesday
Three boys named David and James Forbes and Harry Bennett were charged with throwing stones at the Congregational Church on Sunday last. Bennett admitted the charge, although he was not seen to throw the stone, while the two brothers, who were caught in the act, denied it. The Bench accordingly fin[e]d Bennett 1s. and 2s. 6d. costs, at the same time expressing their approbation of his truthfulness, on the other hand the brothers were each fined 2s. 6d. and 2s. 6d. costs.
(Mercury and Weekly Courier, 24 June 1882)

BRUNSWICK - Wednesday
A man named Haggerty [probably Hegarty] who is well-known at this Court, summoned a neighbour of his, named Skidmore, to show cause why he should not be required to enter into recognizances to keep the peace. Mr. Grylls, who appeared for the defence, informed the Bench that his client denied *in toto* having given the complainant any provocation whatever.

Complainant went into the witness-box, and after being duly sworn, deposed as follows:- "About nine o'clock on Monday morning I was in Hope-street, Mr. Skidmore came up on a horse, I said to him – 'Good morning, Tom'. He then said – 'What game is this you have been up to putting my horses into Henderson's paddock.' I said that I did not do so. He then said to me – 'You did.' I said – 'Come up to Henderson's' but he wouldn't come. He then said to me – 'I'll kill you and your son.' I'm afraid of my life. If I wasn't I wouldn't come here to-day and lose my day."

To the Police Magistrate. "I have no malice

whatsoever. I would do Skidmore a good turn even now."

Cross-examined by Mr. Grylls: 'I swear upon my solemn oath that I am afraid. I swear upon my solemn oath that I never challenged Skidmore to a fight. I swear I did not challenge him to fight one night this month between ten and eleven o'clock."

Mr Grylls: "Now, be careful, we have witnesses here."

At this point the complainant looked about the Court, looked up at the ceiling, pulled down his vest, and adjusted the collar of his coat.

Mr. Grylls: "Will you swear that you did not challenge my client to fight?"

No answer.

The Police Magistrate: "Can't you answer the question? Be careful. Did you challenge the defendant to fight?"

Witness, after a long pause: "No, I did not."

Cross-examination continued: "I made use of no bad language towards Skidman [sic]. I was always friendly with him till Monday morning. I never said to him – 'Skidmore, you are no man if you don't come out and fight. I know a lad named Cannington. I see him now in Court. If Skidmore is fined I will pay the fine for him. Mrs. Skidmore never ordered me out of her home. I do not know Mrs. Davidson. I never told Mrs. Davidson that I'd punch Skidmore's head."

The complainant called his son, a lad of about fourteen years, who deposed that on Monday morning he saw the complainant and defendant in Hope-street, and that the defendant appeared to be talking wicked. Witness could not hear what defendant was saying. This closed complainant's case.

Mr. Grylls called a boy named Farrington who deposed to having heard complainant make use of bad language towards the defendant, and also heard complainant challenge defendant to fight. This witness further deposed to having heard Mrs. Skidman [sic] order the complainant to go away.

The Bench at once dismissed the complaint.

(Mercury and Weekly Courier, 15 July 1882)

BRUNSWICK - Wednesday
Insulting behaviour.

Ernest Fairhurst, on remand from last week, responded to his bail in order to answer the above charge preferred against him by Constable Stewart. Mr. Madden appeared to defend Fairhurst, and Mr. Grylls for Constable Stewart, who deposed that on the 29th ultimo he was on duty in Sydney-road opposite Stewart-street, was talking to a Mr. Lucas about 9 o'clock p.m., when he heard someone yelling and shouting; he proceeded to the spot whence these sounds came, and saw the defendant who was waltzing about on the footpath with his arms extended. The constable remonstrated, saying "my boy, this is very bad behaviour." Defendant replied in a most insolent manner, asserting that he had done nothing wrong and that he would do so again. He was not afforded the opportunity to carry out his intentions for Stewart forthwith run him in. He was, however, subsequently bailed out. In the cross-examination an attempt was made to show that the arresting constable was drunk, but although Stewart admitted to the bench that he had a drink in the previous part of the evening, all the eloquence of the defending counsel failed to prove the fact of intoxication on the part of the constable… Ernest had to suffer a fine of £1 with £1 7s 6d costs.

Street Rowdyism.

John Walker and Joseph Thompson were charged by Sergeant O'Shannasy with fighting, and otherwise misconducting themselves in the public street. Constable McKenzie, sworn, said "I recollect Saturday the 19th ultimo, was standing near the Scotch church. I saw an immense crowd in front of the Brunswick hotel; I repaired to the scene and found that the two defendants now before the court had been fighting. I did not see the fight, I saw the window of Mr. Rodan's shop in which two large panes of glass had been broken during the combat. I believe the cost of the panes to be 15s each."

Sergeant O'Shannassy, sworn, said "I remember Saturday, August 14. I saw Walker, who came to the police station in company with another man. His face was bruised, swollen, and bleeding, and, in fact, he presented the appearance of having been very much punished. He told me that he would institute proceedings against Thompson."

As he had failed to do so, the police took the matter in hand, and the defendants now appeared before the bench to answer the charge preferred against them. Walker, who pleaded not guilty, informed the bench that Thompson came to him in the bar of the Brunswick hotel and accused him of having stigmatized him all over Brunswick, accompanying the accusation with a challenge to fight, which being declined, Thompson struck Walker and a fight ensued. The bench considered that Thompson was the aggressor, and accordingly fined him £1 with 2s 6d costs, in default seven days' imprisonment. He elected to "take it out." Walker was discharged.

A Waif

Louisa Abraham, a pretty little girl of about 4 years of age, was brought before the bench charged with being a neglected child. Remanded for a week.

(Mercury and Weekly Courier, 9 September 1882)

INQUEST: ACCIDENTAL DEATH

Mr. Candler, the district coroner, held an inquest at Brunswick, on Tuesday, on the body of John Skidmore, aged six years, who was found dead in a tank full of water between 4 and 5 o'clock on the previous afternoon. The deceased was playing about the tank with his cousin, when he accidentally fell in and was drowned. The jury returned a verdict of accidental death.

(The Argus, 15 November 1882)

A STRANGE CHARACTER

Death has removed from our midst one of the most eccentric residents of Brunswick. Last Sunday week, Arthur Oliver, or Albion-street east, was found dead in his bed – heart disease being the cause of his death. Deceased was a very eccentric and distant man, the only person living with him being a boy, as servant. Last week deceased frequently complained of pains over the region of his heart, but refused to consult a medical man.

Last Sunday, not having risen with his customary earliness, his servant went to his room to call him to breakfast, when he found he was dead. The police and a doctor were immediately summoned who, on their arrival, found life quite extinct, and from appearances he must have been fully twenty-four hours' dead before the entrance of his servant to his room.

The residence of deceased is one of the prettiest spots in the borough. It is situated in Albion-street, below Lygon-street, and it seemed the hobby of the unfortunate man to keep it in as great a state of cleanliness and novelty as it was possible to do. The garden surrounding the premises is the best for miles round, statues, seats, fountains and ferns are scattered about in every direction, and flowers of the most beautiful kinds send their perfume over the whole place; those in the conservatory are of the most costly and rarest kinds.

Not only is the front portion of the premises paid attention to, the rear being, if anything, more picturesque than the front. At the back door is an immense gum tree, and at a height of fully 40 feet is erected a look-out, with telescopes placed in position from which a view can be obtained for a score of miles round. The fernery, which is also in this spot, is a treat to see – being a regular fern-tree gully.

The interior of the house is complete. The furnishing and other embellishments are superb, and of the most costly kind. There is a piano, harmonium, and other musical instruments – each of which the deceased could play with the touch of an artist.

The strangest part of all is, that with all the cleanliness and order which prevails, we hear that a woman has never been seen within his premises. He was a true misogynist and consequently a misogaimst [misogamist, presumably].

It is related that a neighbour of his had several children who were, or he imagined were, a considerable annoyance to him. He complained several times, and threatened to do everything but what was right to them. Some time after the house of the parents of these children caught fire and was burnt to the ground, and being in straitened circumstances a subscription was got up by the residents to re-build the dwelling. One of the collectors called on Mr Oliver, expecting to be treated with the disdain and loftiness for which he was credited, but what was the surprise of the collector to be asked into the place of the deceased, and without any trouble to be presented with a £5 note.

Deceased was a man of considerable means, but lived almost akin to an Anchorite. He took no interest in public affairs, not even attending a place of worship.

(North Melbourne Advertiser, 17 November 1882)

BRUNSWICK - Wednesday

Illegal detention.

Mary Speakman v. Charles Archer – Illegal detention of property. Mr. Croker who appeared for the defence, submitted that the complainant being a married woman, and having no separate estate could not sue in her own name, her husband should have been made a party to the action. The bench coincided with that view and dismissed the complainant.

(Mercury and Weekly Courier, 3 February 1883)

THE BRUNSWICK BANK ROBBERY

The prisoner George Sweeny, alias Trent, alias Palmer, alias Disant, who was arrested recently in Sydney upon information forwarded from here on the charge of the robbery of £711 10s.1d. from the Bank of Australasia at Brunswick, was brought up at the City Court on Saturday last, he having arrived per train the previous night in charge of Detective O'Callaghan.

On the case being called, the officer named applied for an adjournment for a week, and also that the case might be heard in Melbourne instead of at Brunswick, as it would be more to the convenience of all engaged if this were done. The prisoner made no remark or objection and the remand as asked for was granted. It appears that the prisoner is the man who entered Middleton's American Clothing Factory, at Sandhurst, some time ago and stole goods and money therefrom.

He was identified at Messrs. Parry and Mackay's on Saturday morning as the man who cashed a cheque with them that was subsequently found to have been stolen from the Sandhurst factory. As be passed through Albury he was identified as having cashed stolen notes there, and he has also been identified as having cashed stolen notes in several metropolitan banks.

(Illustrated Australian News, 13 June 1883)

BRUNSWICK BUSSES

By BOZ

It is an old saying that "slow and sure wins the race." I have no hesitation in backing the Brunswick busses and horses, against any other similar mode of travelling in the known world. It is now a common thing for passengers to be an hour on the road, between the city and the royal suburb, simply because the horses are unable to perform the work quicker. The fact is, the nags are broken down and unfit for any other district except Brunswick, whose inhabitants are a peaceful, quiet, contented lot of people, who grumble about nothing – except the 'busses. The drivers who by the way are most obliging and attentive, have become quite job-like in their demeanour, and instead of using bad French and German jargon, ply the whip with a vigor that would astonish any horse whose hide was thinner than cast iron.

The want of keen competition on the Sydney Road, in passenger traffic, is the cause of the present most unsatisfactory and disgraceful state of affairs. On every other line there [is] a "cabby" who keeps the bus company in a perfect state of good management, but the unfortunate people of Brunswick are at the mercy of the company who [to] show their appreciation for the magnificent returns obtained from the residents, send out the greatest "old mokes and broken winded horses" they can collect in the colony.

In Hotham, South Yarra, Collingwood, Carlton &c., the horses are in good condition, and do their trips with ease and quickness, but not so to and fro from Brunswick. The attention of cab-men should be directed to the present wretched state of affairs, and if they undertake to run out, in say, forty-five minutes, allowing six of seven stoppages at the various water troughs for a drink, they will soon get custom, and do good service to the travelling public of Brunswick.

(North Melbourne Advertiser, 15 June 1883)

BRUNSWICK COURT

Four small boys named Cornwall, Trenoweth, Sedgement and Codeley were summoned for stealing vegetables from Mr George's garden. Mr George described the damage done to his garden, and stated that although the actual value probably only amounted to 5s, he would not have taken £5 for the damage done. The offence took place on last Sunday during church time, when the young urchins amused themselves by uprooting vegetables, etc... The young delinquents all admitted the offence, and Mr George asking the bench not to make the punishment too heavy but

that a good lecture might be administered to them instead. They were let off with a fine of 2s 6d with [unclear] costs.
(North Melbourne Advertiser, 29 June 1883)

AN ELECTION ASSAULT CASE

An action was brought in the Melbourne County Court Monday, before his Honour Judge Cope and a special jury of four by Mortimer Murphy Ginane, a carter of bricks at Brunswick, against William Davis, rate collector of the same place to recover £99 damages for assault. At the last general election, on the 22nd February, plaintiff was doing electioneering work for Mr Pigdon, the unsuccessful candidate for East Bourke Boroughs, and defendant, who was roll clerk there, was a supporter of Professor Pearson, the successful candidate.

From the evidence for the plaintiff it appeared that after the election, at half past six o'clock, plaintiff was walking down the street at Brunswick, when he met the defendant, who turned round and said, 'We have beaten you today,' when plaintiff replied, 'Yes, you have; but perhaps you may not do it again.'

Plaintiff followed this up by calling defendant an Orangeman, with an opprobrious epithet prefixed. Defendant then raised a heavy stick he was carrying and said to plaintiff, 'Take that you ----- Papist,' and struck him violently over the temple, rendering him insensible, and inflicted such injuries that he was unable to work for five weeks. Plaintiff said he lost about three quarts of blood, and in cross-examination he admitted that the called the defendant a ----- Irish dog.

Dr Michael Dominick Murphy, who attended Ginane subsequent to the assault, deposed to the injuries received, there being a large wound over the temple which had bled very much. Mr MacDermott appeared for the plaintiff, and Messrs Purves and Hood for the defendant.

The evidence of the defendant and his witnesses flatly contradicted that for the plaintiff, it being stated on oath that the plaintiff was drunk, that he had been in an excited state during a considerable part of the day, and that he commenced the assault by calling Davis foul names, prodding him in the back with a stick, and subsequently striking him over the head with it.

The case was before the County Court some short time ago and on that occasion His Honor entered a nonsuit on account of the contradictory nature of the evidence. Yesterday, a verdict for the defendant was returned by the jury, and His Honor directed that costs be taxed. Mr MacDermott gave notice of appeal on account of misdirection of the judge.

(Kerang Times and Swan Hill Gazette, 29 June 1883)

SUICIDE AT BRUNSWICK

A painful case of suicide occurred at Brunswick some time during Wednesday night or Thursday morning. A man of about 60 years of age, named Ralph Smith, was found dead in the stable at the rear of his brother-in-law's premises, Mr Joseph Clarke, a saddler and news agent, Sydney-road. Deceased was first discovered by a young man, in Clarke's employ, named Oaks, who, on going to the stables at six o'clock, on Thursday morning, found Smith on the floor of the feed house, leaning against a partition with his head on one side.

He tapped him and said, "Come, old man, this is a cold place for you to sleep in," but receiving no reply, he again tapped him, and on stooping down found he was dead, and noticed a rope with a running noose round his neck, the extreme end bearing appearances of having been broken.

Constable Jackson, who was on duty, was called in, and the body was removed into the house. Deceased was collector of dog fees for the borough of Brunswick, but so far as can be ascertained, there is nothing wrong with his accounts.

(Mercury and Weekly Courier, 8 September 1883)

THE WAR IN BRUNSWICK

At the Brunswick Court on Wednesday, the 3rd instant, before Mr. Shuter, P.M., His Worship the Mayor (Cr. Methvin [Methven]) and Messrs Stranger, Tinning, and Harrison, a young man named Charles Fitzgibbon was charged with insulting behaviour in a public place with intent to provoke a breach of the peace. Mr. Maddock appeared for the prosecution, and Mr. Snowball defended the accused.

The first witness called was Mr. Charles Crook, a member of the Brunswick Borough Council, who deposed [as] follows: "I am the Secretary of the Independent Church, Brunswick. I was at the church on the evening of the 28th September. The Salvation Army was holding a meeting it was not open to the public. It was what is called a holiness meeting and was open only to members of the army and to good Christians. I was standing in the porch, a young man named Buckingham was acting as door-keeper. The prisoner came to the door and called out "War Cry". He was not selling the *War Cry*.

"Buckingham told him to go away but he said he would not go. I then told him to go away and as he refused to go I took hold of him by the shoulder to put him out. A struggle then ensued and we both went down. I called to some people to give me a hand to put him out, and we put him out. He then went into the road and picked up some stones and threw them. He wanted me to fight but I told him to go away and that I was not a fighting man. After a while he went away some distance and then came back again.

"I went to look for a constable but could not find one. The prisoner then ran away I went into the church. In about half an hour I heard a disturbance. I came out and went over to him and said I would detain him until a constable came. He then walked away towards the bus stables. I followed him and he was then arrested by a constable who found a stone in his pocket."

Cross-examined by Mr. Snowball – "I am not a member of the Salvation Army. The prisoner said he had as much right to be in the church as I had, but such is not the case. The rowdy element is not admitted. It is easy to know that element. The church is in my charge. I am positive the prisoner was in the church. He was on the step. He was half in and half out."

Constable Kepfelt, deposed to having arrested the prisoner on the evening of the 28th September. Witness had no warrant. Was not sure what he arrested the prisoner for but supposed it was for assault. Supposed Sergeant O'Shanassy could answer the question.

Mr. Maddock said that was the case for the prosecution.

Mr Snowball submitted that the case had not been proved. He said the evidence was vague and indefinite, and further that the Salvation Army was a body that caused a very great deal of discord.

Mr. Maddock objected to Mr. Snowball making that statement unless he could prove it. No evidence to that effect had been given.

Mr. Snowball would not press that point but he would say that Mr. Crook was not the proper person to make the complaint. He was not the doorkeeper and had interfered when he had no right to interfere…

The prisoner then made a statement to the effect that upon the day in question he met some friends and had some drinks with them. He was not used to drink and it went into his head. He had no recollection whatever of having gone to the Independent Church upon the evening of that day, but if he had done anything wrong he was very sorry for it. He had lost his employment with the 'Bus Company, and he hoped the Bench would take that into account.   The Police Magistrate said the prisoner had committed a very serious offence for which he could be severely punished, but taking into consideration that he had lost his employment, the Bench would not inflict as heavy punishment as they would if such had not been the case. The prisoner would have to pay a fine of £3 with £2 2s. 6d. costs, or in default be imprisoned for one month.

(Mercury and Weekly Courier, 13 October 1883)

SUNDAY LIQUOR TRAFFIC IN BRUNSWICK

To The Editor, Sir –

I was perfectly staggered in reading the report of police proceedings in [t]his borough last week to find the magistrates dismissed several cases of Sunday liquor selling. I do not suppose that there was ever clearer evidence submitted in support of the offence, and certainly it is quite time some steps were taken to put an end to the disgusting sights we have to witness in our streets, and around some of the public houses on the Lord's Day.

It is simply disgraceful to have law and order set at defiance in our midst, and to show sympathy towards such conduct in a court of justice after the recent proceedings, d[e]mands rigid enquiry. I trust the police will still persevere, and should a similar scene be enacted, it will be necessary for the ratepayers to consider what steps should be taken to vindicate the law, and assist the police in their endeavors to rid our streets and dwellings of such nuisances, and save our young men from the downward course such temptations put in their way.

Trusting to have your able advocacy in this matter. I am, &c.,

AN OLD RESIDENT.

(North Melbourne Advertiser, 28 December 1883)

POLICE INTELLIGENCE

At the Brunswick Court on Wednesday...Henry Humphry was charged with bathing in the Merri Creek, contrary to the bye-laws of the borough. Repeated complaints had been made to the police of the number of boys bathing in the creek and disporting themselves on the bank in a nude condition in the view of the residents of the vicinity. As his was the first case of the kind this summer a light penalty was inflicted, and he was fined 5s., and 2s. 6d. costs.

Timothy Lynch proceeded against his father, John Lynch, for unlawful assault. On Monday prisoner attacked his son in a savage manner, and threatened to kill him. The son had to lock himself in a room for safety, and after swearing an information had the father arrested, as he was in danger of his life. Prisoner was remanded for a week to be examined by a medical man, as it is believed that he is insane and unfit to be at large.

The borough inspector proceeded against 20 persons for allowing cattle to wander over the borough. Fines varying from 5s. were inflicted in each case.

(The Argus, 24 January 1884)

BRUNSWICK BOARD OF ADVICE
Lively Proceedings.

The usual monthly meeting of the above board was held in the State school last Tuesday evening. Present – Messrs Stranger (chairman), George (correspondent), Clark, Strickland, Fleming and Boase. After the minutes of the previous meeting had been read and confirmed, the teacher of the night school was invited into the room. He stated he had of late been annoyed by a number of larrikins who seemed to take a delight in throwing stones on the school roof and otherwise causing much annoyance. He asked the board to write to the sergeant of police, reporting to him the circumstances with a hope that a policeman would be told off to suppress the present nuisance.

Ordinary Business.

Mr Fleming said the first business for the meeting was the election of a chairman. Mr Stranger he said had filled the position for nineteen months and he considered that was long enough to satisfy any reasonable man. As it was the proper time and also the first meeting since the squabble, he moved that a new selection be made.

Mr George at once proposed that Mr Stranger be re-elected. He considered Mr Stranger had given satisfaction to all the members.

Mr Fleming contended there were others who had a

perfect right to the position and he considered it was very unfair to again place Mr Stranger who had held the chair for nineteen months.

Mr Clark said he had no fault to find with Mr Stranger nor objection to offer and he would therefore second the motion.

Mr Fleming maintained it was wrong and to test the meeting he would propose that Mr Boase be chairman.

Mr Boase declined.

Mr Stranger said he had no desire to again occupy the chair as it had not been a bed of roses.

Mr Fleming "Ugh! Neither will it be!"

Mr Stranger thanked the members for again re-electing him.

Mr Fleming objected to the resolution on the grounds of already holding the position for over a year and a half.

Mr. George said that had nothing to do with the matter.

Mr Stranger hoped that all squabbles were now over. [W]as then declared re-elected.

The Minutes

Mr. Fleming drew attention to the fact that a copy of a certain letter ordered to be sent to the department did not appear in the minutes. He asked the correspondent to read the letter.

Mr George "It was read at the last meeting."

Mr Fleming "No it was not, I will show how you carry on your little game, when a letter like many others of importance is required, it cannot be found when wanted."

The chairman – "If these interruptions are going on we had better adjourn and consider what is best to do with Mr Fleming."

Mr Fleming – "Yes, you had better adjourn, and you will then want to know what to do with my solicitor."

Mr Clark – "Mr Chairman, are we going to transact any business or not, if not I'm going home."

The matter then dropped.

Correspondence.

From Mrs Fourdinier complaining that she had received a summons for not sending her daughter to school as required by the Act, although she had written to the head teacher explaining her daughter was ill.

Mr Strickland enquired if the Act expressed that a teacher was expected to file all excuses and notes for parents, if not, the board could do nothing. It was the duty of the truant officer to ascertain the reasons and not the head teacher.

Mr Fleming – "Oh the board wants another investigation."...

Resignation.

Mr Strickland – "Mr Chairman is this all the business.

Mr George – "Yes."

Mr Stickland – "Then allow me to hand you my resignation."

The members – "Oh no."

Mr Strickland – "Yes I find that matters are not as pleasant as they should be, and I have therefore decided upon this course.["]

Mr Strickland was desired to withdraw his resignation but refused. He then retired wishing the members "good night."

Mr Strickland's action and firm resolve caused a quietness of some moments, the members seeming to be greatly surprised.

Caretaker.

Mr Fleming said he had heard that Mr George had made some strange statements respecting the conduct of the caretaker to a member of the daily press with a view of having them inserted, but which were not correct.

Mr George after a short warfare with Mr Fleming said he would explain. He said a person employed on the premises was found drunk and a member of the board had taken her home. He thought it was a disgraceful affair and a letter should be written to Mr Hayden on the matter.

Mr Fleming – "Did you say that it was the caretaker and that she was only paid 10s per week while Mr Hayden was receiving 30s from the government. I am prepared to state she was not the caretaker or charwoman and that she was not drunk, and therefore you ought to be more careful about your statements when making them to the reporters.

Mr George – "I've been very uneasy about you of late."

Mr Fleming – "Well you will be very much more uneasy about me before long."

In response to Mr George, Mr Boase said he was in Frith-street and saw a woman who was a stranger to him sitting on the kerbstone she was evidently under the influence of drink. She had a bottle, but the beer had run out, and a little boy belonging to the Salvation Army said "Here woman here's a *War Cry* it's better than beer." He raised her up and took her to the school, where he found it was not the caretaker who expressed great sorrow to him at seeing her mother in such a state.

Mr George thought the circumstances were shameful, and Mr Hayden should be apprised of the facts. Such conduct should not be tolerated and the minister would never allow it…

The meeting which was of a most extraordinary character and which in some passages defies description adjourned for a month.

(North Melbourne Advertiser, 15 February 1884)

BRUNSWICK POLICE COURT

At the Brunswick Court on Wednesday – before Mr Akehurst P.M., Messrs Straw, McDougall, Stranger, Fleming, Tinning and Harrison, J.P.'s.

William McCann, who had been arrested on warrant, was brought up on remand charged with unlawfully assaulting James Hede, inspector for the borough of Brunswick. The Bench inflicted a penalty of £5, with £5 5s. costs, in default three months' imprisonment.

Hede then proceeded against a man named Robert

Potter for using threatening language. In this case, as in the previous one, Hede had summoned Potter for allowing his cattle to wander. Defendant met the prosecutor last week and abused him in a fearful manner, threatening to "do for him" if he ever summoned him again. The defendant was fined £2 with £1 3s. 6d. costs, in default 10 days' imprisonment.

Charles Mallen was charged by the truant inspector with neglecting to cause his children to attend school the requisite number of days in the quarter. Defendant had been fined several times previously for the same offence, but still neglected to send his children to school. The Bench inflicted the heaviest penalty allowed by the act – viz., £1 in each case, with 2s. 6d. costs, to be levied in distress.

Ann Simpson was charged by Margaret Williams with using obscene language. The prosecutor stated that the defendant, while in a drunken condition, stood at her door in a perfectly nude condition and used most filthy language in the hearing and view of persons passing. Defendant did not appear, and a fine of £10 was inflicted, or three months' imprisonment.

Matthew Walsh, teacher of the Roman Catholic school, was charged by Senior-constable Brown with unlawfully assaulting Frederick Gaspard. From the evidence adduced it appears that on Sunday week Gaspard, who is an Industrial School boy boarded out to Mrs Ryan, went to Sunday-school wearing some artificial flowers in his coat, which Walsh requested him to remove. He impertinently refused to do so, whereupon the defendant punished him rather severely. The Bench dismissed the case, at the same time stating that the punishment was greater than the offence merited, but it was difficult to put themselves in the place of a teacher.

(The Argus, 21 February 1884)

MYSTERIOUS AFFAIR AT BRUNSWICK

A case of supposed murder was brought to light at Brunswick about 2 o'clock yesterday afternoon, the dead body of a woman being found in a clay-hole attached to the premises of Mr. Alfred Cornwell, pipe manufacturer, situate[d] in Phoenix-street, and within 20ft. of the new railway line, and close to the Sydney-road.

It appears that on Wednesday some boys living in the vicinity, on returning from school, saw what they thought to be a bundle of rags floating on the water. Not attaching any importance to the matter, they did not mention the subject to anyone, but one of the boys, in passing again yesterday, seeing the bundle in the same place, but not exactly in the same position, thought he distinguished the head of some person. He immediately took off his clothes, and pluckily swam to the object, and brought it to the bank. He hastily dressed, and informed the police of the affair.

Constables Bourke and Mahony were on duty on the Sydney-road, and were quickly in attendance. They made a careful examination of the body, which was found to be of a woman about 22 years of age. She was dressed in a light red-coloured print dress, two cotton and one flannel petticoats, a pair of dark woollen stockings, and a pair of odd kid boots. Several marks of violence were found on the body, one on the left cheek, which seems to have been caused by a blow from a fist or some blunt instrument. There is also a bruise on the right cheek near the throat.

The cause of death is believed to be suffocation, one of the woman's cotton petticoats having been drawn up and twisted round her throat. The mark on the right cheek seems to have been caused by the woman being roughly dragged along the ground by the petticoat after death, and the body placed in the hole where found. Although a diligent search has been made, no trace of the woman's hat can be found.

The face of the deceased was quite black. It is almost impossible for the case to be one of suicide, for had the deceased wished to commit self-destruction in all probability she would have at once thrown herself into the water, which is about 10ft. in depth, and the tightening of the petticoat at the back of the neck, instead of under the chin, is also against the supposition of suicide.

The appearance of the body shows that it has been in the water for about a week. The deceased is a perfect stranger in Brunswick, about one hundred persons having viewed the body, none of whom can identity her. The body was removed to the Cumberland Arms Hotel, where an inquest will be held.

(The Argus, 1 March 1884)

A CHURCH DISPUTE – STRANGE SCENES

Matters in connexion with the Brunswick Baptist Church have latterly been in a very disturbed state, owing, it is stated, to the action of some of the more prominent members and deacons in refusing to pay their usual contributions towards the support of the church and pastor, with the intention of compelling the latter to resign his position.

Last Sunday fortnight Mr Shalberg, before commencing his sermon, stated that he had a very painful duty to perform, and one which he had kept from the public as long as possible, but that the innocent should not suffer with the guilty, he had determined to bring the matter before the congregation. He stated that owing to the conduct of some of the wealthy deacons in withholding their contributions he had been unable to pay his way, and had consequently become involved. He named several of the deacons personally.

Before Mr. Shalberg had time to conclude his statement a scene of the greatest confusion took place. Several of the deacons whose names had been mentioned, walked up to the pulpit in a threatening manner, and gave Mr. Shalberg's statement the lie direct. On the following Monday evening, a meeting of the congregation was held in the Mechanics' Institute, and a resolution passed and forwarded to Mr. Shalberg to the effect that the members present had every confidence in him, and offering to provide him with a church in the district.

Matters during the past fortnight have been more settled, Mr Shalberg having vacated his place in the pulpit, which has been supplied by a stranger, but on Tuesday night a more serious disturbance took place. It appears that the rev. gentleman during his stay in the district had opened a branch of the Blue Ribbon Army in connexion with the Sunday school. At the monthly meeting on the evening named he was advertised to deliver a lecture in the building, which is occupied by an arrangement with the trustees and the army, who pay a nominal rent.

At 8 o'clock, the time for the lecture to commence, the members to the number of about 200 had arrived, only to find that a padlock had been placed on the gate which leads into the yard. The pastor jumped the fence, and with his key opened the door. Then he found that the gas had been cut off. The members and adherents present demanded entrance, particularly as they had not received any notice, that the usual meeting should not take place. The padlock was finally removed from the gate and a rush was made for the church.

In the darkness and confusion Deacon Burton accidentally struck Deacon Jenkins in the face, the latter, thinking the blow was meant for the pastor, and with the intention of saving him from that indignity, lifted his hand to ward it off, planting a severe blow, in the action, on the cheek of a Mr Wilson, who was standing near. The minister and his intended chairman then left the scene. We understand that a meeting of deacons is to be held this evening, to consider the relations with the minister, who has, it is stated, resigned his position.

(The Argus, 27 March 1884)

INFANTICIDE IN BRUNSWICK

The dead body of a newly-born female child was discovered early yesterday morning in an old clay hold situate[d] off Hope-street, Brunswick, by some children passing on their way to school. They took the body, which was floating on the surface, to be that of a dead dog, but on closer examination one of them discovered that it was that of a baby. They informed a neighbour of the discovery, who immediately sent word to the police.

Constables Williams and Jackson proceeded to the hole, and, recovering the body, removed it to the lockup, where an inquest will be held this morning. The body when found was quite naked, and had been in the water for about a week, and, from appearances, seems to have been born near the spot and thrown into the hole, no trace whatever being left of the perpetrator of the deed.

(The Argus, 9 August 1884)

BOARDS OF ADVICE - BRUNSWICK

At the meeting of the Brunswick Board of Advice on Tuesday evening a very warm controversy took place with regard to a complaint of Mr. H. Walkerden, which had been referred to Mr. Hayden, the head master, for a report thereon. Mr. Walkerden complained that his daughter, a girl verging on fifteen, had been ordered to stand upon a form for a very trivial offence, and that the girl having been instructed by her mother not to do so, refused to comply with the order, upon which the master had expelled her from the school for disobedience.

Mr. Hayden's report commenced by stating that complainant's statement was "totally untrue," and then went on to explain the facts, which fully bore out the complaint of Mr. Walkerden. His statement also alleged impertinence and defiance of the order given.

A section of the Board were inclined to accept Mr. Hayden's report as final and justifiable. Another section of the Board were dissatisfied, and considered further inquiry was needed, owing to the contradictory nature of complaint and report, especially as the Walkerdens were known as respectable, well-conducted people, besides being of opinion that it was indecent and an immodest thing to make a well-grown girl of that age to stand on a form in front of a lot of boys of nearly similar age, which of course was the same view of the case as held by the mother, and eventually carried a motion referring the matter to the Secretary of the Board of Education for further inquiry.

The motion was carried by the casting vote of the chairman (Mr. T. Stranger), who was supported by Messrs. Clark and George, while Messrs. Tough, Purves, and Lacey voted against it.

(Mercury and Weekly Courier, 13 December 1884)

BRUNSWICK POLICE COURT

At the Brunswick court on Wednesday, before Messrs. George (mayor), Fleming, Talbot, Tinning, and Rose, J.P.'s, Margaret Power was charged with resisting the police in the execution of their duty. Constable Paice stated that a woman named O'Connor had fallen and broken her leg in a brawl. Dr Talbot attended to the woman, and advised her removal to the hospital.

The witness was about to convey her there, but Mrs. Power would not allow him to move her, and struggled with him most violently. In the fight the defendant fell on the fractured limb of Mrs. O'Connor, causing her great agony. The Bench dismissed the case, as they considered that the defendant had acted as she considered best for her friend, at the same time remarking that the police had only performed their duty in forcibly taking the woman to the hospital.

(The Argus, 5 February 1885)

BRUNSWICK COURT

Elizabeth Snowden v William Snowden. The complainant told the Bench a most pitiful tale of domestic misery and alleged that her husband had illtreated her for years and she was afraid of her life. She wanted him bound over to keep the peace as she thought he would do her some harm.

The defendant alleged that his mother-in-law had aggravated him without any cause and his wife had threatened to blacken his eyes and 'do' for him on the first opportunity. He then cross-examined his wife asking her some questions quite unfit for publication. In answer to the Bench the defendant said that there were two children the result of the marriage. He lived on his wits and his means as a good many others did, and was a surveyor by profession. The Bench bound him over to keep the peace for twelve months in his own surety of £50 and two of £10.

Patrick McNamara was charged will illtreating Elizabeth Egan, a child boarded out with him from the Industrial Schools. It was alleged that he sent the girl for some beer and because it was a little thick he beat her unmercifully with a heavy strap. He was fined £5 with £2 14s costs.

Elizabeth Shannon, licensee of the Quarry Hotel, was charged by Mr. O'Connor, Chief Inspector of Excise, with placing liquor in a bottle bearing the label John De Quyper. On the 24th of last April Inspector Reidy visited the defendant's hotel and found a bottle of gin bearing De Quyper's trade mark exposed in the bar for sale. He examined the contents and in his opinion it was not genuine and he then informed the licensee that it had been tampered with. A daughter of the licensee then admitted she had put a little water in the liquor. Mrs. Shannon would not accept payment of the bottle neither would she seal it. The strength of the genuine article was proof and the stuff in question was 22 under proof. The offence was admitted by Mr. Grylls who appeared in answer to the charge said he asked that as his client was a widow a nominal penalty only would be inflicted. After a long consultation the chairman announced that they had decided to inflict a penalty of £5 with £2 2s costs. The result caused a little surprise as Mr. O'Connor had only asked for a small fine and costs.

(North Melbourne Advertiser, 3 July 1885)

FATAL ACCIDENT AT BRUNSWICK

On Friday forenoon, the 21st inst., a terrible machinery accident occurred at the No. 2 Hoffman's Brick Company's works, Brunswick, the sufferer being a youth sixteen years of age named John Delahunty. The unfortunate lad was employed clearing out the dirt from underneath one of the rolling tables, when he lost his hold of the shovel, and, in endeavouring to regain it, became entangled in the powerful machinery, the result being that his right leg was torn away above the knee joint.

Delahunty was at once carried to the company's office, pending the arrival of Drs. Elliott and Talbot, who recommended his immediate removal to the Hospital, which was effected after a tourniquet had been applied to the injured limb. It was then found that he was suffering from compound [unclear] fracture of the thigh and other serious injuries, which had a fatal termination. He never rallied, but died shortly after his admission at a quarter to one p.m.

An inquest on the body was held at the Hospital, on Monday, by the city coroner, Dr. Youl. Mr. Leonard appeared to watch the case on behalf of the friends of the deceased. Sub-Inspector Brown was present on behalf of the police. Albert Hore, a laborer in the employ of the company, deposed that he was working with deceased on Friday. The[y] were employed in receiving bricks as they were made from the machine. The machine was worked by steam. Deceased had a shovel in his hand, which got caught in the machine. In trying to extricate the shovel he got caught himself, and received the injuries that proved fatal.

There was no protection to prevent the laborers going too near the machinery. Witness considered the occurrence accidental. William Dalziel, engine driver, gave evidence that he considered the machine sufficiently protected. He had to stop the machine to get the deceased out. He was caught by the knee. Michael Bowden's evidence was that the deceased was caught by the revolving table. He was caught by the knee, and in order to be caught in that position he must have left his proper post. The machine was as well protected as it possibly could be to do the work. (A model of the machine was here produced, and the witness explained the working.) He was cross-examined by a number of jurymen.

The foreman at the works, Peter Wagner, deposed that the machine had been working for fifteen years without a similar accident having occurred. He thought the machinery was not dangerous. In answer to Mr. Leonard, the witness said it was possible to protect the machinery where the deceased was caught, but as no person had occasion to go near there, it was not thought necessary to protect it. The Coroner in summing up considered that the machinery was not unduly exposed. The jury after a short consultation returned a verdict of accidental death, and added a rider to the effect, that the jury were of opinion that the machinery should be better protected.

(Mercury and Weekly Courier, 28 August 1885)

BLACKGUARDISM IN BRUNSWICK

Certain evidence that came before the Brunswick Police Court on Wednesday last, showed conclusively that the Borough is sadly in want of increased police protection, and that the long talked of police station at East Brunswick could not be established one moment too soon. It was clearly proved that on last Sunday afternoon, half-a-dozen grown up larrikins of the most pronounced type – downright unmitigated blackguards – were amusing themselves in one of the most crowded thoroughfares by throwing stones at houses, windows, lamps, &c., and were varying the amusement by plastering peoples dwellings with mud. One thorough young vagabond 'shied' a stone at a lamp that cost £5. The stone struck the lamp, smashing it in pieces.

At the meeting of the Council on Wednesday evening, Cr. Methven drew a terrible picture of the doings of the local blackguards. Windows broken wholesale in every direction, and rotten eggs thrown into people's houses. Language of the most disgusting character to be heard upon every side. The worthy councillor animadverted in severe terms upon the conduct of the local magistrates who, instead of "making it a caution" to blackguards convicted of insulting behaviour[,] obscene language, wilful damage to property, &c., let the offenders off with ridiculously inadequate punishment. In his (Cr. Methven's) opinion it was about high time to try and put a stop to such disgraceful conduct.

(Mercury and Weekly Courier, 2 October 1885)

BRUNSWICK COURT

A young man named Charles Selby was charged with indecent exposure on the previous Saturday afternoon. A girl named Maria Littlejohn gave evidence that as she was returning home on the afternoon of the date mentioned, the prisoner who had his dress disordered followed her and behaved in a disgraceful manner. On reaching home she at once told her mother and the prisoner was subsequently chased by her father and a youth named O'Hara who overtook him in Victoria street when he asked to be leniently dealt with as he was a gentleman and an architect of the city.

On being confronted with the girl she accused him of having acted in an indecent manner and chasing her all the way home. The prisoner denied this and stated that he was merely running through the fields for exercise which he had been recommended to take by his medical adviser. His shirt was hanging out through a large hole in an old pair of trousers he had on at the time and the whole thing had been misconstrued by the girl. The Bench failed to agree upon a verdict.

(North Melbourne Advertiser, 4 December 1885)

BRUNSWICK COUNCIL

At the last meeting of the above Council, at which all the representatives were present, the following extraordinary proceedings took place, which for 'originality' may be classed happily amongst the things that do not occur every day. It appears that the Public Works Committee met on the previous Wednesday to transact the ordinary business, which, however, was set on one side or considerably neglected to take advantage of the opportunity to oust Cr. Fleming from the position of chairman. On grounds which have not yet transpired the majority removed Cr. Fleming, who was naturally rather wroth, and expressed his dissent in most emphatic protests.

Cr Fleming certainly lacks discretion, and is too free with his tongue, which is the great stumbling block in the way of his usefulness, but it is going beyond reason when a majority of colleagues determine they will 'gag and sit' on their chairman because he occasionally uses language more forcible than polite, yet often 'very straight and to the point.'

It unfortunately happens that when a public man, in the eyes of his fellows, becomes, in their minds 'officious', or 'crotchety', the result is the formation of a clique that on every occasion, like the actors in the bull ring, throw up dirt and goad on to further scenes and troubles. Such conduct is despicable, and deserves the censure of onlookers, who love fair play, justice, and proper local government as against snarling and spitefulness and local neglect, were the same amount of time devoted to improving the streets, removing nuisances, and otherwise attending to the sanitary warts of the borough, it would be more satisfactory to the burgesses and more creditable to their representatives. The result of the committee's action is so unique that a public meeting should be called to consider the whole question...

(North Melbourne Advertiser, 29 January 1886)

BRUNSWICK SEVERANCE DISPUTE

A large deputation of the Brunswick ratepayers was introduced to the Minister of Public Works (Mr. Nimmo) by Professor Pearson last Friday with reference to the petition for severance presented by the residents of West Brunswick, who in consequence of the unsatisfactory progress of the borough, desired to be separated from the eastern portion and form a separate municipality with the Sydney road as the boundary line. The ratepayers on the east side of the borough objected to the severance and were also present to lay their views before the minister...

Mr. Melville stated that he spoke as a ratepayer and not as a parliamentary representative. He had been a resident of Brunswick for thirty years and was strongly in favor of severing the West from the East as the best way for each side to advance. The petition was signed by a large majority of the residents of West Brunswick and those in the east were really not interested as they were not property owners on the other side. He urged that the borough was unfairly divided into wards and the revenue most unevenly distributed. In consequence of the division and frequent disputes in the council hardly any business was transacted and the roads were left to go to ruin although time after time efforts had been made to get the council to repair them. Accidents were of frequent occurrence and many people had left the district through the wretched state of affairs. In his opinion severance was the only remedy and unless it was granted their properties would become valueless. If severance was granted a saving of 20 per cent on road metal alone could be affected.

Mr. Rose J.P. pointed out that persons who had purchased land in the north west portion of the borough, could not build on it because there was no water through the council's dilatoriness in neglecting to proceed with reticulation works. Water from the street channels had actually to be used by householders.

Cr. Leithhead (Coburg) alleged that the previous loans had been comparatively wasted and the minutes of the council would show the extraordinary procedure. Mr.

Stranger J.P. and Mr. John Breeze also spoke strongly in favor of severance.

Cr. Crook (Mayor) opposed the petition and contended that if the borough was divided, serious difficulties about drainage and in connection with the tramway would arise. The council was endeavouring to float a loan which was what the borough wanted instead of separation. He contended that the petition had been got up by several would-be councillors. The council had desired to make cross roads in West Brunswick, but were unable to do so because they had been blocked by land syndicates.

Mr. Fitzgibbon also objected to the severance, principally on account of the council having failed to carry out its promise, to erect the Moonee Ponds Creek Bridge on certain land given by his wife conditionally for the purpose, and until this was satisfactorily settled he would protest against any severance. The interview was a most stormy one, and the speakers were frequently angrily interrupted, so much so that the Minister [said] that if any further personalities were indulged in, he should have to dismiss the deputation.

Mr. Melville's reference to land syndicates and to the proposed loan, which he termed a "nefarious loan," produced quite an uproar, several persons speaking together, and making it very difficult for the Minister to understand the real wishes of the ratepayers. He at last declined to hear any more, and intimated that he would give his decision shortly.

(North Melbourne Advertiser, 28 May 1886)

SINGULAR GUNPOWDER EXPLOSION AT BRUNSWICK

A singular accident happened at Brunswick early on Sunday morning to a man named Johnstone, residing in Brunswick-street east, by which he sustained injuries of rather a serious nature. It appears that on Saturday his wife, while proceeding with her domestic duties, found a flask containing a quantity of gunpowder in one of the rooms. To put it out of the way, she placed it in the grate, intending to remove it out of the room, a circumstance which she unfortunately neglected to do.

Early the following morning her husband determined to place a fire in the grate, and proceeded to the room with a shovelful of live coals, and threw them into the fireplace. A loud explosion instantly followed, scattering the articles in the room, and stunning Johnstone and burning him about the face and hands. Dr. Henry was sent for, and examined Johnstone, and found that he had escaped being dangerously hurt, the shock to the system being the most serious. The force of the explosion exhausted itself up the chimney otherwise the sufferer would have been much more seriously wounded. The report was heard for a considerable distance, and attracted a number of the residents to the spot.

(The Argus, 8 June 1886)

LARRIKINISM AT BRUNSWICK

At the Brunswick Court yesterday four youths named Joseph Delaney, Christopher Davidson, Thomas Roche and Angello Danelli were charged with unlawfully assaulting two Chinese named Ah Sam and Ah Cheong, market gardeners. Mr Grylls appeared for the prosecution, and upon his application the charge against Danelli was withdrawn. Mr Hodges appeared as interpreter.

From the evidence it appeared that the defendants were in Moreland-road, and in passing the Chinamen's garden Davidson threw a stone, striking Ah Sam on the back. Other stones were also thrown. Ah Cheong and Ah Sam then went on to the road to ask the reason of the assault, when they were attacked by Delaney and Davidson, the latter striking the Chinamen in the face with a whip, which he had in his hands.

Information was given to the police of the assault, and a summons was issued. Delaney, who had just previously been fined £5 for obscene language, and who received a bad character from the police, was fined £5. Davidson, who had also been previously before the Court, was also fined £5, and Roche £2 10s., the costs being fixed at £1 3s. 6d. in each case. In case of default of payment, the defendants will be imprisoned for seven weeks.

A number of young men were charged with using obscene language, and in the majority of cases heavy penalties were inflicted. The Bench are fully determined to support the police in their endeavour to put a stop to the practice, as it is becoming almost impossible for young ladies to pass along the streets without listening to the disgusting language used...
(The Argus, 17 June 1886)

THE FATAL RAILWAYS ACCIDENT AT BRUNSWICK

Mr. Candler, the district coroner, held an inquiry at the Brunswick Hotel, Brunswick, yesterday morning, concerning the death of John Francis Hecking, aged 40 years, an iron turner, who was killed at the level crossing at Union-street, on the Brunswick and Coburg railway line, on last Saturday evening, under circumstances of a very painful character, the deceased being killed before his brother's eyes. The scene had such an effect upon the brother that ever since the occurrence the latter has been in a most critical condition and in a constant state of delirium, and was unable to attend to give evidence at the inquiry yesterday.

The first witness examined was Thomas Reilly, gatekeeper at the crossing, who deposed that on the evening of the 11th inst. the deceased and his brother were running to catch the train, which was just entering the station beyond the gates. He called out to them to stop, but they did not hear him. The surviving brother succeeded in crossing the line, but the deceased was not so fortunate, being knocked down by the engine and thrown on to the line. The whole of the train passed over him, and when witness went up to him he was quite dead. The train was punctual to time, and the gates across the line were closed, the deceased entering through the small wicket-gate. The driver of the train blew his whistle, when approaching the station, and also called out to the deceased, but could not prevent the accident. People were in the habit of running the risk of being run over by crossing the rails in front of the engine when approaching the station, and he was powerless to prevent them. There was no automatic apparatus attached to the gates, and if there had been in all probability the accident would not have occurred.

Arthur Roach, the stationmaster, stated that a similar accident occurred at the crossing about nine months ago, but it did not end fatally. He was not aware of a regulation preventing persons crossing the line when the gates were closed. The crossing was a very much frequented one, about 300 persons a day passing over it.

John Bent, the engine driver, stated that he blew his whistle when approaching the station, and when at near the crossing saw one man cross over the line, followed by the deceased, who was only about three yards from the buffers. He applied the brake, but was unable to prevent the accident, which was due to the fault of the deceased. The practice of crossing the line when the gates were closed was very common on the suburban lines, and he had often to pull up to save people.

Dr. Cutts described the injuries of the deceased.

The Coroner, in summing up, stated that these level crossings were a source of danger to the public, and the number of fatal accidents happening on them was alarming, for although gatekeepers warned the public, they would attempt to cross in front of the train, regardless of all danger. The jury returned a verdict that the deceased was killed by being accidentally run over by a train at the level crossing at Union-street; and added a rider to the effect that the gates should be closed automatically, which recommendation the coroner intimated he would forward to the Railway Commissioners.

(The Argus, 15 September 1886)

CURIOUS ACCIDENT

A peculiar accident happened at Brunswick at about 3 o'clock yesterday morning. A large underground drain is being constructed in Union-street for the purpose of carrying the storm water from the Sydney-road. The excavated material is thrown on to the side of the street, and makes an embankment of a great height, which considerably interferes with the traffic.

A dray loaded with wood was coming along the road when the horse shied, rushed on to the embankment, and capsized the dray. The horse was quickly released from its awkward position, and rushing over the banked earth, fell into the excavated channel, a depth of about 15ft., landing on its feet, the hole just being of sufficient size to accommodate it.

After about three hours' hard work the animal was lifted out of the excavation. The novel sight attracted a great crowd during the time preparations were being made for the animal's release, which was accomplished with blocks and tackle.

A young man who was working at the bottom of the hole had a most marvellous escape, the horse, in falling, striking him on the head and knocking him down, bruising his shoulder rather severely.

(The Argus, 27 October 1886)

SHOCKING SUICIDE

A man named Alexander Wilson Harvey committed suicide at East Brunswick on Friday morning, at 8 o'clock. The man has been drinking heavily of late, and on Wednesday evening he suffered so much from delirium tremens that the landlady, Mrs. Watkins, residing in Weston-street, and a fellow lodger named Gorman, were obliged to remain with him the whole night.

Some time after seven o'clock Harvey became easier, and Mrs. Watkins and Gorman left him, thinking he would soon recover. After a few minutes the landlady returned surprised to find the unfortunate man lying under his bed, bathed in a pool of blood. The main arteries and the windpipe were cut so severely by a razor as to almost sever the head from the body.

An inquest was held, when it transpired that deceased was born at Falkirk, Scotland, has been employed as an ironmoulder at [obscured] Foundry, East Brunswick, for the last five or six months, and was a terrible drunkard. He was about 28 years of age, and had neither friends or relatives in the colony.

The jury returned a verdict to the effect that Harvey committed suicide while of unsound mind.

(*The Age, 11 January 1887*)

"NORTH MELBOURNE": DISORDERLY MEETING

A meeting was held at the mayor's room, town-hall, Brunswick, last evening, called by advertisement in *The Argus*, of ratepayers who supported the action of the mayor and seven councillors in seeking to change the name of Brunswick to North Melbourne. The room was crowded to excess.

Mr. J. C. PHILLIPS, who announced himself as the convener of the meeting, stated that he could see that the meeting was a rushed one, and as convener of the meeting he would declare it closed. The meeting had been packed by those who desired to vote in a certain way. The invitation was issued to those who were desirous of procuring a certain point. The closing of the meeting in this way was objected to by those present, and a scene of great confusion ensued.

Mr. J. TRENOWITH was subsequently voted to the chair, and the business was proceeded with.

The CHAIRMAN said that he did not see the use of the meeting being called. The Minister of Public Works had decided not to give the name either to Brunswick or Hotham, and he took it that the matter was finally settled.

Mr. J. LACEY quite agreed with the remarks of the

chairman, and moved that it was not desirable to change the name from Brunswick to North Melbourne. It was mentioned that but for the brickyards and quarries Brunswick would be a second Toorak. It was the brickmaking industry that had built up Brunswick – a name which was known over the whole of Victoria. Take away the name Brunswick, and they took away its prosperity. The movement was an endeavour to strike at the root of the industries of the district.

Mr. BARNGHAM seconded the motion. Both speakers during their addresses were continually interrupted, and scenes of great confusion took place.

Mr. TUCKER moved as an amendment that it was advisable to alter the name to North Melbourne. Although the Minister had declared that he would not alter it, they would fight until they succeeded. The sitting Minister was only a creation of today. The argument that all title deeds would have to be altered was nonsense, as at the present time some of the deeds of Brunswick properties described them as being in Melbourne.

Mr. PHILLIPS seconded the amendment, when another great scene of confusion and disorder followed. He said that this matter had been taken by a side-wind. He and his supporters cared not what a chance resolution did. A house-to-house canvass of the ratepayers would be made, and a petition prepared to be presented to the Minister, and the majority should rule in this matter. They would not be put down by a packed meeting. If he was in the minority he would bow gracefully to the majority.

Mr. STRAUKS [probably Stranks] also spoke in favour of the amendment.

The CHAIRMAN stated that he was in favour of the change, but he had taken the Minister's decision as final. He did not believe that if a petition were presented to him the Minister would re-open the matter.

Another scene of great uproar followed, the chairman being quite unable to control the meeting or put the resolutions. After some time, during which matters were becoming worse, he declared that as they would not allow him to proceed with the business he would declare the meeting closed.

Mr. PHILLIPS, addressing the reporters present, stated that the whole meeting was a fiasco and simply rushed, and that the matter would subsequently be settled by a house-to-house canvass.

The chairman subsequently announced that the meeting was adjourned till next Thursday.

The meeting throughout was of a most disorderly character, speakers addressing each other in a most excitable manner, personalities being indulged in to the detriment of order and legitimate business. Both inside and outside the building a considerable amount of feeling was shown.

A vote of thanks was accorded the chairman.

(The Argus, 4 February 1887)

ALLEGED GAR[R]OTTING AND ROBBERY AT BRUNSWICK

An elderly man named William Woods, a builder and contractor, has reported to the Brunswick police that on Thursday evening he was garrotted and robbed of the sum of £53 and a silver watch. Mr. Woods states that on the evening of the day in question he had visited several hotels, at which he had imbibed rather freely, and that he had the money stated in his possession. While at one hotel he paid for his drinks with a £20 note, which was changed for him, after which he started for his residence, which is in a lonely and distant part of the borough. The time was about 10 o'clock. He alleges that when he was near Margaret-terrace he was struck on the head from behind, and knocked down and robbed of the amount stated, together with the watch.

Mr. Woods complained severely of the pain occasioned by the blow, which he states was delivered with great force. The police have been making every endeavour to discover the thief, but up to the present have not been successful. Wood was not sober when the offence was alleged to have taken place.

(The Argus, 5 February 1887)

ATTEMPTED SUICIDES AT BRUNSWICK

An old man named Michael Maloney, aged 82, a stonemason by trade, residing at East Brunswick, made a deliberate attempt to commit suicide at about 1 o'clock on Sunday morning, but was detected in the act. It appears that the man, who was residing with his son-in-law, left home at about 9 o'clock on the morning in question, having quarrelled with his daughter. As he did not appear at dinner time, information was given to the police, and a search was made for him.

After some delay he was found on the edge of an abandoned quarry-hole, at the rear of the East Brunswick state school, which was full of water, and of a great depth. His hands and feet were securely tied with cord, and he was about to spring into the hole when he was secured by a man named Tinkle, and detained until Constable Mahoney arrived, and took him to the East Brunswick Police Station. A letter was found upon him stating that he was drowning himself, as his sons would not support him, a statement which the police say they know to be incorrect. The prisoner, who is a very feeble old man, was brought before Mr. Straw J.P., at the Brunswick Court yesterday morning, and remanded till Wednesday.

A man named Thomas Farrell, a labourer, residing in Wilson-street, Brunswick, made an attempt to commit suicide yesterday afternoon. Farrell had been attacked with typhoid fever in a very bad form, and was being attended to by Dr. Elliot, who recommended his removal to the Melbourne Hospital. He was taken there yesterday morning and refused admission, as the place was overcrowded. He was conveyed back to his home, and soon after arriving there he was attacked with delirium, and, evading his watchers, he secured a large piece of broken bottle, and made a great gash in his throat, which bled profusely, but which is not dangerous. Dr. Talbot was quickly called in, and attended to the man, who, as he was very violent, had to be placed in a strait-jacket. Last night he was somewhat recovered.

(The Argus, 8 February 1887)

FATAL ACCIDENT AT EAST BRUNSWICK

An accident of a melancholy character, and which ultimately had a fatal termination, happened at East Brunswick at about 8 o'clock on Saturday morning to an old resident of the district named William Sergeant, aged 60 years. It appears that at the time mentioned the deceased was in the bar of the Quarry Hotel, at the corner of Weston and Lygon streets, and had some refreshments. It became necessary for one of the members of the licensee's family to go down the cellar to tap a hogshead of beer, and in order to prevent people entering while the cellar remained open, the bar door was locked. The customers inside were also warned about the open cellar, particularly Sergeant.

The deceased suddenly had his attention drawn to something passing outside, made a rush to the door, and in doing so he fell down the open cellar, a distance of 7ft. falling upon his head. The men in the bar rushed to his assistance, and brought him to the top, when he was found to be in an insensible condition... The deceased never gained consciousness, but gradually sank, and died at about five o'clock the same evening. The medical officer gave a certificate of death, rendering an inquest unnecessary. The deceased leaves a widow, but no family.

(Kyabram Union, 4 March 1887)

DISORDERLY MEETING OF THE BRUNSWICK COUNCIL

On Wednesday evening the Brunswick Borough Council adjourned several important items in order to allow the councillors to entertain Mr. Burrell, the town clerk, previous to his departure on his two months' leave of absence. Amongst the adjourned business was a motion standing in the name of Councillor Fleming to the effect "That tenders be called for laying steel tracks in Union and Albert streets." This resolution came on for consideration last evening, but several councillors objected to it on the ground that the matter was already under the notice of the public works committee.

Councillor Fleming, as mover of the motion, was introducing the subject, when suddenly Councillor George exclaimed that Councillor Fleming had called him "a downright liar" and a "lying scoundrel". Considerable tumult ensued when Councillor Fleming refused to withdraw the objectionable words.

Councillor George then requested the mayor (Councillor Clement) to have the words taken down, but the mayor declined to comply, as he stated that he did not hear the remarks uttered.

Further confusion arose, and ultimately the excitement and the uproar grew so intense that the mayor threatened to leave the chair, and was in the act of doing so when Councillor George arose and addressed the mayor thus: "You ought to leave the chair if you do not do your duty. It is a miserable piece of work if you cannot enforce order. You are utterly unworthy to occupy the position of mayor to allow a councillor to act in this way. You encourage Councillor Fleming to make a disturbance night after night." These remarks added to the already heated feeling.

Councillor Methven considered that were Councillor Fleming to be left more to himself he would not say things at the council table for which he was afterwards sorry. But it was the habit of several councillors to be always snarling at him, and finding fault with him. Councillor George did everything he could to irritate Councillor Fleming; in fact, between these two councillors a constant feud of enmity existed, which frequently cropped up at the table.

Councillor George said he had borne insult after insult from Councillor Fleming which no other councillor would have stood.

The mayor was on the point of making an explanation, when the whole of the councillors, with the exception of Councillors Fleming, Methven and the mayor left the council table, the council thus breaking up in disorder, and allowing several important items on the notice-paper to lapse.

(The Argus, 15 April 1887)

GAR[R]OTTING AT BRUNSWICK
    A Mrs. Allen reported to the Brunswick police yesterday that while passing along Albert-street on the previous Saturday night, she was knocked down by a man, who stole her purse and contents. She screamed, but the cowardly fellow decamped upon hearing footsteps. A description of the offender has been furnished.
    (The Argus, 19 April 1887)

THEFTS FROM SHOPS AT BRUNSWICK
    At the Brunswick Court yesterday morning, before Messrs. Clement (mayor), Crook, and Straw, J.P.'s., a respectable-looking woman named Elizabeth Sampson and her daughter, a little girl aged about 13 years, were charged with larceny. It appears that on Saturday evening the prisoners, in company with another woman, were observed examining the goods in front of the drapery establishment of Mr. J. Hutchinson, Sydney-road, and the elder prisoner was detected picking up a roll of flannel and placing it in a perambulator, which was in the charge of the young girl. The material was carefully covered up, so as to convey the idea that a child was in the carriage, and the women made their way along the Sydney-road.
    Information of the theft was given to Mr. Hutchinson, who followed the women, and overtaking them found in the perambulator, in addition to the flannel, a piece of velveteen, which had also been stolen from his shop. Sergeant Brown, who was in the vicinity, arrested the girl, but the elder prisoner escaped, but was subsequently arrested at her residence at Albion-street after a desperate resistance. Upon a search of the premises being made, numbers of other articles which are supposed to have been obtained in a similar manner were discovered, one being a large roll of flannel, which has been identified by Mr. Belot, draper, as having been stolen from him only a few days previously. Other shopkeepers have also complained to the police of the mysterious disappearance of portions of their stock.

The prisoners were remanded until Wednesday, bail being allowed in two sureties of £50 each.
(The Argus, 26 April 1887)

INQUEST: INFANTICIDE AT BRUNSWICK

Mr. Johns, the deputy coroner, held an inquest at the Quarry Hotel, Brunswick, on Monday afternoon, upon the body of a male child which was found dead upon the previous day upon a vacant allotment of land in Weston-street, wrapped in a piece of damask cloth. Constable Bourne stated that he found the body about 9 o'clock on Sunday morning, and that it was quite dead. Dr. Louis Henry stated that he made a *post-mortem* examination of the body. He found that the child, which was about 24 hours old, had been born alive. It had been partly washed, and death was caused by suffocation. The jury returned a verdict of criminal neglect, after birth, by some person or persons unknown, which is tantamount to a verdict of wilful murder. The police are investigating the matter, with a view of discovering the guilty persons who placed the body where it was found.
(The Argus, 17 May 1887)

DISORDERLY SCENE IN THE BRUNSWICK COUNCIL

A very disorderly scene took place at the meeting of the Brunswick borough council last evening owing to the conduct of Cr Fleming. On the business commencing, Cr Fleming immediately took objection to a letter which had been sent by authority of the public works committee, and shortly afterwards a letter was read from a ratepayer, requesting the levels of Glenlyon-street.

An acrimonious discussion followed, and Cr Crook being frequently interrupted whilst speaking to the question by Cr Fleming, who referred to him as "Crooked Charley", requested the mayor to "keep this drunken man in

order." The discussion proceeded as follows: -
    Cr Fleming: "Who's drunk?'
    Cr Crook: "You are."
    Cr Fleming: "I am not drunk, sir."
    Cr Crook: "I say, Mr Mayor, he is not fit to sit at the council table."
    Cr Fleming: "Withdraw that remark, sir."
    Cr Crook: "I'll not withdraw it."
    Cr George then moved that the council adjourn for half an hour, which was seconded by Cr Cadman and carried.
    Shortly after resuming, Cr Fleming rose, together with Cr Cadman, to speak to a matter of drainage.
    Cr Fleming: "Sit down, Cr Cadman, I am in possession of the chair, and am before you."
    A voice: "With your tooral, looral."
    Cr Crook moved – "That this council consider the conduct of Cr Fleming at the council table most disorderly."
    Cr Cadman seconded the motion, which was carried, two councillors refraining from voting.
    Cr Fleming continuing to address the chair, the mayor said he could not allow him to speak until he apologised and withdrew his remarks.
    Cr Fleming ignoring the ruling of the mayor, Cr George moved and Cr Crook seconded, "That the council adjourn." The motion was carried and the meeting dispersed amidst a scene of the greatest disorder and disruption.
(The Age, 28 September 1887)

ATTEMPTED SUICIDE AT BRUNSWICK
    A married woman named Elizabeth West, residing at Edward-street, Brunswick, made a most deliberate attempt to commit suicide yesterday morning, and, but for the timely arrival of a neighbour, the attempt would have been successful. It appears that about 10 o'clock Mrs. West left the house and proceeded to a stable in the yard, procured a rope, threw it over a beam in the building, placed her neck in a running noose, and lifting her feet from the ground,

attempted to strangle herself.

Mrs. Kent, residing next door, wishing to see Mrs. West, went into the house, and not finding her in, went to the stable, and found her in the position described. With great presence of mind she lifted her from her dangerous position, and cut the rope, which was drawn tightly round her neck, the woman being nearly dead and quite unconscious. Mrs. Kent then applied remedies to restore her, and after some considerable time succeeded.

Information was then sent to the police, who took the unfortunate woman in charge, and also sent for Dr. Talbot, after which she was removed to the Hospital. No reason can be given for the rash act, as the woman is in very comfortable circumstances and highly respected in the neighbourhood where she resides; but it is stated that she had previously made an attempt to destroy herself.

(The Argus, 9 November 1887)

REMARKABLE CASE OF ABDUCTION: A YOUNG GIRL CARRIED OFF FROM BRUNSWICK

A most peculiar case of abduction occurred yesterday afternoon at Brunswick, a young girl of weak intellect being enticed away from her friends and carried off to the city in an audacious mariner. So successfully was the offence carried through that up to a late hour last night the child had not been recovered, nor had her abductor been arrested, though the police were informed of the matter shortly after it occurred, and took immediate steps to spread such information as would lead to the detection of the offender, and the return of the child to her family.

The child in question is named Rose Roache. She is 12 years of age, and her father is a corporation labourer. The mother is dead, and an elder sister takes charge of the children, there being a family of five. Rose, owing to her weak intellect, has been an object of special solicitude. She was playing with several others near the house at about 2 o'clock, when a young man in the dress of a midshipman, who had been observed loitering about for a short time previously, asked a little girl of the party to go away with him, at the same time showing her some money. She ran away from him, and he asked one or two others, but could not prevail upon them to accompany him.

Rose Roache would appear to have taken refuge in the house, and the man prevailed on a little boy (her brother) to enter the house and induce her to come out. She did so, and the man entered into conversation with her, and they walked away together. Finding that they did not return, the other children gave information of what had occurred to the elder sister, and she, after a hurried search, became alarmed, and gave information to Sergeant Brown, of the Brunswick police station, who instantly set inquiries on foot, and telephoned to Russell-street barracks, as well as to Port Melbourne and Williamstown.

The man was about 18 or 20 years of age, of fair complexion, with a fair moustache, and he wore, as before stated, a midshipman's uniform, namely, white trousers, blue jacket, and cheesecutter cap with a gold band. He was well dressed and very neat in his appearance, whilst the child was rather poorly clad in a light brown dress and straw hat trimmed with blue velvet.

She is of fair complexion, with hair inclined to curl, and her eyes have a vacant, wandering expression, which indicated the condition of her mind. Such an ill-assorted pair could not fail to attract attention, and they were easily traced to a point on the Brunswick tram line, about half a mile distant from the child's home. Here the trail was lost, and it was concluded that the man had taken the child with him on a tram to Melbourne. At a late hour last night this surmise was verified, for inquiries amongst the tram conductors elicited the fact that Conductor Howell had noticed the man and the child get on to the dummy of his car at half past 2 o'clock. He was struck by the contrast in their appearance, and wondered if the ill clad child could be the sister of such a smart looking person, and if not why she should be travelling in his company.

On the way to town the man volunteered the remark

that it was three years since he had been in Brunswick before. The man left the car at the Post-office, in Elizabeth-street, taking the girl with him, and no further trace of the pair has been discovered.

Mr Roache and his elder children are in great distress. A sister, who is out at service, came home on hearing the news, and was so much overcome that she fell into a fit which lasted for a considerable time, and added to the tribulation of the unfortunate family. If the man is a midshipman it is not likely that he will take the child to any seaport where he would be known. The police in the city and suburbs will be on the look-out, and aided by the full description which has been furnished, and the peculiarities of the dress and appearance of the pair, should soon be able to give an account of them.

LATER: The girl was arrested by the police early this morning, and placed in the Little Bourke-street lock-up, where her father shortly afterwards called.

(The Argus, 30 December 1887)

LARRIKINISM AT BRUNSWICK

Catherine Hegarty, Amelia Weisa, William Kerwood, and John Montgomery were brought before the Brunswick Bench yesterday on a charge of insulting behaviour. Constable Williams stated that he observed the defendants creating a disturbance opposite the Wesleyan Church on Saturday evening. When witness appeared they at once dispersed, but they afterwards reassembled, and were guilty of gross misbehaviour on the Sydney-road. The girls were stated to be a pest to the district, but nothing was previously known against the youths. Weisa and Hegarty were each fined £5, and the lads 40s., the default in each case being one month's imprisonment.

(The Argus, 5 April 1888)

CASE OF POISONING AT BRUNSWICK

Mr. Frederick P. Fitzgerald, aged 29, a chemist, carrying on business at Sydney-road, Brunswick, poisoned himself yesterday morning under peculiar circumstances. The deceased, who recently commenced business in the district, having arrived from Newmarket, retired to bed at about 11 o'clock on Monday evening in his usual health, but during the night be became very restless, and could not sleep.

At about 4 o'clock in the morning he got up, went into the shop, and prepared a sleeping draught, which he took. His wife arose at about 8 o'clock in the morning, when he was apparently well, except shivering with the cold. She left the room for a short time, and when she returned he was moaning heavily. Dr. Overend was sent for, and soon after his arrival Fitzgerald died. An inquest will be held on the remains this morning. The deceased leaves a wife and two young children.

(The Argus, 27 June 1888)

MYSTERIOUS AFFAIR AT BRUNSWICK

An elderly man named William Werrett, very old resident of Brunswick, and residing in Holmes-street, died in the Melbourne Hospital on Saturday under peculiar circumstances. It appears that on the evening of the 25th ult. the deceased was drinking at the Edinburgh Castle Hotel, and reached his home, which is in rather a distant part of the district, at about 2 o'clock on the following morning, in a semi-unconscious condition, with a large cut on the head and other bruises.

He was questioned by his wife as to how he sustained the injuries. He at first stated that he had been assaulted by larrikins, but afterwards said that nobody had injured him. He remained unconscious all night, and on the 27th ult. Dr Stewart was sent for, and upon examining the man he found his wounds to be of a very serious nature, and advised his immediate removal to the hospital, which was done. On the following day the medical man also reported the matter to the police, who investigated the affair.

No information whatever could be obtained to clear up the mystery, and it is not known whether the man sustained the injuries by a fall, or whether he had been set upon and assaulted. The police carefully examined the roads leading into Holmes-street, which Werrett would take on his way home; and in Albion-street, near the Salvation Army's Prison Brigade Home, they discovered a pool of blood near the edge of the gutter, and it is suspected that the accident, or whatever it may have been, occurred at this spot. Upon inquiries being made from persons in the vicinity, it appeared that nobody heard cries on the evening of the date of the affair. The matter as it at present stands, is a mystery, and no light whatever can be thrown upon it.

(The Argus, 2 July 1888)

INQUEST: THE SUICIDE AT EAST BRUNSWICK

The district coroner held an inquest at East Brunswick yesterday on the body of the woman Mary Ann Orchard who committed suicide on Sunday morning by shooting herself.

George Orchard, a carter, deposed that the deceased was his wife, and was 47 years of age. He missed her on Sunday morning about half-past 4 a.m. On searching he found her in the feed-house dead, with a revolver under her foot. She must have obtained the revolver from under his pillow, where he had been accustomed to put it for the last three months. The deceased had been low spirited, but never showed any sign of any intention to take her own life. She was very temperate.

William Orchard, son of the deceased, deposed that he was with his father when he found the body in the feed-house. He believed his mother had shot herself.

Dr. Aitchison deposed that he had made a *post-mortem* examination of the body. The cause of death was a pistol-shot wound in the head. He was of opinion that it was inflicted by the deceased herself. The deceased had been under his care for three or four weeks past, and, though she was rational when he last saw her, from the appearance of the organs of the body he was of opinion that she was not of sound mind.

Mary Ann Hackward deposed that she lived next door to the deceased, and had known her for about five years. She had been strange in her manner of late, and her mind seemed going. On Friday last she told witness that she would jump into a hole and drown herself some of these days. Witness did not tell Mr. Orchard.

The jury found that the deceased died from a pistol shot wound in the head inflicted by herself while of unsound mind.

(The Argus, 11 September 1888)

SHOOTING ACCIDENT

Yesterday evening, about 6 o'clock, a married woman, named Alice Moloney, 22 years of age, residing in Donald-street, Brunswick, was accidentally shot in the hip by her husband. Mrs. Moloney was making tea and her husband was loading a revolver which he keeps for shooting the goats that get into his garden, when, by some mishap, the revolver went off and the bullet struck Mrs. Moloney in the hip. She was brought to the Melbourne Hospital and admitted as an in-patient, but the wound is not considered serious.

(The Argus, 5 December 1888)

A HUSBAND KILLS HIS WIFE

A fatal shooting accident, under most painful circumstances happened at East Brunswick early on Saturday morning. A man named Thomas Maher, a carter, who resides in Weston-street, East Brunswick, went to a ball held under the auspices of the local cricket club on Friday night last. He was accompanied by his wife, a young woman 21 years of age. After the dance was over they were returning home with a neighbour named Mrs. Chivers, who resides in John-street, when they picked up in the street a small revolver wrapped up in a silk handkerchief. At the gate of the Mahers' residence Mrs. Chivers said good-bye, but she had not gone very far when Maher came running after her stating that he had accidentally shot his wife.

It appears that when they went into the house Maher took out the revolver which he had found and was examining it, and Mrs Maher was taking off her hat at the dressing table. She noticed that he had the revolver in his hand, and remarked that it was too small. She did not think it could be of much use. Without looking in what direction the muzzle was pointing, and not knowing that it was loaded, he pulled the trigger twice without any result. The third chamber happened to be loaded, and as the cartridge exploded his wife cried out that she was shot.

He hurried away for a doctor, and after some delay obtained Dr Hamilton who advised the woman's removal to the Melbourne Hospital where she was admitted. Mr. E. M. James, who attended her, found that the bullet, which was only about the size of a pea-rifle one, had entered her abdomen and perforated the intestines. With some difficulty he abstracted it, but all hope of saving the woman's life was despaired of from the first. After the operation she was exceedingly weak, but yesterday revived sufficiently to allow of her living depositions being taken. This was done by Mr Williams, the secretary of the Hospital, in the presence of the husband.

The woman's statement was merely a repetition of the facts already given and she was most emphatic on the point that the whole affair was accidental. The depositions were taken about midday, and she lingered on till 8 o'clock last night, when she expired. She was only 24 years of age, and leaves two children one of whom is little more than an infant.

(The Argus, 9 September 1889)

ALLEGED BURGLARY AT BRUNSWICK: AN EXCITING CHASE

At the Brunswick Court yesterday a young man named George Kelland was charged with entering the premises of Charles Lawrence, news agent and tobacconist, and stealing goods valued at £15.

From the evidence adduced it appeared that on the evening of the 2nd inst. the prosecutor, who carries on business at Sydney-road, North Brunswick, had occasion to leave his shop, and on returning at 3 a. m. found that the back door had been broken open, and a silver watch, together with a quantity of tobacco, had been stolen. About 5 o'clock the same morning the accused, in company with two others, was seen by Constable McIntyre walking towards the city in Madeline-street, and on being stopped said that he was a milkman.

All of them were carrying parcels and as the constable approached the other two decamped, and all made good their escape. They dropped the parcels, however, which contained tobacco and cigars, afterwards identified by Lawrence.

The following morning the three men were met by Constable McIntyre in Swanston-street, and he immediately gave chase. They all ran in different directions, and the constable followed Kelland, who ran through Latrobe, Little Lonsdale, Elizabeth, and Franklin streets, and there managed to escape. Constable Gaynor then came up, and from the description given him, arrested the accused shortly afterwards whilst hiding amongst some cases in the yard belonging to Messrs. Munro and Co. A plant of tobacco was also discovered amongst some bricks on a vacant allotment in Victoria-street, Brunswick. The accused was seen to visit the place the day following the robbery. The prisoner, for whom Mr. Bencraft appeared, was committed for trial.

(The Argus, 17 October 1889)

SERIOUS STREET ACCIDENT

A very serious accident happened at about half-past 10 o'clock, on Sunday night, on the Sydney-road, Brunswick, whereby a man named James Mulley, residing in Albert-street, Brunswick, was severely injured. It appears that at about the hour named Mulley, who is a member of the Salvation Army, was returning from Melbourne, driving a spring cart. He was accompanied by two young women, also members of the Salvation Army, and, when opposite the Presbyterian Church, he collided with a milk-cart going in the opposite direction, and driven by a man named Andrew Kerr.

The force of the collision was so great that the shaft of the cart driven by Mulley entered the breast of the other horse, killing it on the spot. Mulley and the two women were thrown on to the road with great violence. With all speed they were conveyed into a chemist's shop close by, and Dr. Talbot was quickly in attendance. Mulley was found to be the most seriously injured, his arm being broken, and his face much cut, besides being otherwise hurt, his injuries being of such nature that late last night he was in a very precarious condition.

Miss Vincent was most hurt of the two young ladies, having been thrown on to her head on to the road. Last night, she was delirious, but no fatal consequences are anticipated. Miss Miller, the other young woman, escaped with a severe shaking. The driver of the milk cart was unhurt.

(The Argus, 24 December 1889)

FATAL ACCIDENT AT BRUNSWICK

An old resident of Brunswick named James Deeker, aged 72 years, died on Thursday evening from the effects of an accident which happened to him on the previous day. The deceased was standing on a ladder cleaning off bills from a building which had been used as Mr Brunton's committee-rooms on the Sydney-road, and by some means fell from the ladder on to the asphalt footpath underneath. He was picked up in an insensible condition, and conveyed to his home in Charles-street, but he never regained his senses, and died as stated. It is thought that the fall was caused by the deceased becoming giddy when on the ladder. An inquiry was held yesterday, when a verdict of accidental death was returned, the cause being concussion of the brain, besides other internal injuries.

(The Argus, 26 September 1890)

SUICIDE AT BRUNSWICK

A man named Henry Francis Green, aged 34, a saddler, residing at Laura-street, Brunswick, committed suicide some time during Thursday evening in a most singular manner. The deceased, who is a married man, separated from his wife, resided with his mother, and retired to bed apparently in his usual health on the evening named. Not appearing as usual to breakfast his mother went to call him and found he was dead.

It was at first thought that he had died from natural causes, but later in the day it was discovered that he had committed suicide by stabbing himself in the heart with a small sharp-pointed dagger, and having bled inwardly, he had died without a struggle, and without leaving a blood-stain on the bed-clothes. An inquest will be held on the remains today.

(The Argus, 1 November 1890)

UNNEIGHBORLY NEIGHBORS

A peculiar case of assault occupied the attention of the Brunswick Police Court on Wednesday, when an elderly man, named Edward Fitch, proceeded against Alexander Somerville, who appeared before the bench, bearing a couple of medals on his breast, for unlawfully assaulting him.

From the evidence of the complainant, it appeared that on the evening of 11th inst. he was sitting in a room at home, when he heard a knock at the door. His lad went and answered the knock, and as a result got knocked down by defendant, who rushed in and also struck plaintiff, without cause whatever. The parties lived close together, and had not spoken to each other for three days.

Mr Shannon, who appeared for the defendant, asked: Do you drink?

Witness: Oh, I like a glass.

Do you ever get drunk?

Occasionally.

What do you call occasionally. Every day in the week?

No; now and again.

Well, is it not a fact that you get drunk and walk up and down your yard in a nude condition?

No; it is not.

The son of complainant gave similar evidence as to the assault, and in cross-examination stated that he had had a quarrel on the day in question with a son of defendant's, and Somerville, on coming to the door, wished to know why he had struck his son.

Defendant made a statement to the bench that he had been continually annoyed by plaintiff, whose son had thrashed his little boy. He went to Fitch's place to enquire why this had taken place, and was rushed at by the father and assaulted.

A fine of 10s. was imposed, with 13s. costs.

(The Coburg Leader, 5 November 1890)

TRAGEDY AT EAST BRUNSWICK: A GRIEVED FATHER COMMITS SUICIDE

Considerable excitement was created at East Brunswick on Tuesday afternoon when it became known that a man named William Hart had shot himself at the bakery establishment of his son in Lygon-street. Many rumours were at first afloat, one amongst others being that murder and suicide were the principals in the tragedy, but such proved not the case, the deceased having simply ended an embittered life by discharging the contents of a revolver into his head.

Before entering into the particulars of the case it may be as well to state that the deceased resided at Dryburgh-street North Melbourne, and for some time had been on bad terms with his children. At the beginning of this year he caused to be circulated a pamphlet of a villainous nature addressed in the shape of a letter to his eldest son, Frederick William, who he accused of having acted "in an unscrupulous and sneak thief manner," whilst he also launched out in bitter invectives against his youngest son Alfred, and daughter Nellie. On Tuesday afternoon, at about half past one, he appeared at the shop before mentioned, but his son saw him coming and left. Hart then contented himself with warning his daughter-in-law to look out of the way and at once shot himself.

Additional light was thrown on the circumstances surrounding the suicide at the inquest conducted by the District Coroner (Mr. Candler) at the East Brunswick Club Hotel on Wednesday morning. All the relatives of the deceased were present.

Evidence was first taken as to the actual tragedy, the first witness called being Alice Hart, who stated that she was the wife of Frederick William Hart, a baker, carrying on business in Lygon-street. About 1.20 p.m. yesterday her husband saw his father, the deceased, coming in the direction of the shop, and therefore left by the back door. Deceased came to the front door, and after a moment told her to look out. He had a revolver in his hand, which he held up, and witness seized her baby, and rushed into a back room. Almost immediately afterwards she heard a report, and looking out saw her father-in-law fall to the ground. She then went outside and called for assistance, there being no one in the house save herself and child. Deceased had not been on good terms with his family for the past 12 months, and last week warned her husband (his son) to be careful of him. He did not appear to be in his right senses. He was paralysed on one side, but was able to get about...

Margaret Hart, wife of the deceased, stated that... she never noticed any signs of insanity displayed by him, but since the departure from home of the youngest boy and girl he had been very melancholy and thoroughly broken in health and spirits. His whole talk was of their ingratitude, but although melancholy she did not think his mind had been affected or his reason unsettled. Last evening she searched his trunk in company with his daughter-in-law. Written on one of the pamphlets circulated by him concerning the treatment of his children, she found the following, showing that he evidently contemplated suicide: "The treatment of my children, as given in these pamphlets, together with the great pain and suffering of rheumatism and the result of apoplexy, explain the cause of death. –

Wm. HART."...

The foreman desired to know of Mrs. M. Hart if she knew that deceased had been driving around in a cab circulating pamphlets. Witness replied that she was acquainted with this fact. It was useless for her to endeavor to stop him, however. She was certain deceased was not insane. It was simply his illness and poverty that had caused him to commit suicide...

The jury returned a verdict that deceased died from gunshot wounds, self-inflicted, whilst of unsound mind.

(The Coburg Leader, 26 November 1890)

SHOOTING ACCIDENT AT BRUNSWICK

A young man named Percy W. Lloyd, 22 years of age, living at 31 Evelyn-street, Brunswick, was admitted to the Melbourne Hospital last night suffering from the effects of a bullet wound in the head. It appears that Lloyd had gone to spend the evening at the house of a friend named Isaacs – a tailor carrying on business at Sydney-road. Two or three other young men were present, and one of them named Moore, picking up an old pinfire revolver belonging to Isaacs, which was lying on the table, commenced playing with it. The weapon unexpectedly exploded, and the ball lodged in Lloyd's left ear, inflicting a dangerous wound. The wounded man was taken to the Melbourne Hospital and attended by Dr. Soilleux, who reports that he is in a serious condition.

(The Argus, 7 January 1891)

INSULTING BEHAVIOUR

John Quinlan and William Williams, two young men, were proceeded against for this offence. Constable Ivens was the prosecutor, and stated that on Sunday afternoon last a number of young men, including the defendants, were standing at the corner of Lygon and Edward streets. They were acting in an unbecoming manner, and shaking hands with each other whenever ladies were approaching. Constable Mahoney also gave similar evidence, but the Bench held that there was no evidence of an intent to provoke a breach of the peace, and dismissed the case.

(The Coburg Leader, 4 February 1891)

ACCIDENT AT BRUNSWICK: TWO MEN ARRESTED

A boy named Alfred Tospell, aged 13 years, residing with his parents at Victoria-street, Brunswick, met with rather a serious accident at about 7 o'clock on Monday evening. The lad, in company with a number of other children, was playing about some swing-boats and merry-go-rounds, placed on an allotment in Albert-street, near the state school. While the boats were swinging the boy got in the way, and the boat struck him with great force on his head knocking him down senseless. When he was picked up it was found that he was greatly hurt, and he was as quickly as possible conveyed to Dr. Hamilton's surgery, and subsequently to the Melbourne Hospital, when it was discovered that he had sustained a fracture of the skull. The matter was reported to Sergeant Brown, and as he considered that sufficient care had not been exercised by those in charge of the swing-boats to protect children from injuries, and as the boats &c., had been taken down and preparations made for leaving the place, he arrested two men named John Cole and Daniel Pennington on the charge of, through negligence, causing bodily injury to the boy Tospell. The men were admitted to bail in one surety of £100 and their own recognisances of £50 to appear at the next court sitting.

(The Argus, 4 February 1891)

LARCENIES AT BRUNSWICK

The town of Brunswick has been for some time past visited by an expert gang of thieves and housebreakers, scarcely a day passing during the past month without robberies having been reported to the police. In addition to the cases of horse-stealing already referred to in *The Argus*, numerous larcenies have taken place.

The thieves, instead of now taking horses, have diverted their attention to harness-stealing, three cases of such a character having occurred last week. On Thursday night the stable at the residence of George Leister, of George-street, was entered, and a new set of buggy harness, valued at £8, stolen; and on the previous night a similar robbery was committed at Ernest Knight's, when several articles of harness, valued at £3, were stolen. Mary Hodgson, of Edward-street, also reported to the police the theft of a silver watch and chain, valued £7, from her residence on Thursday night.

Notwithstanding that extra vigilance is exercised by the police, no trace whatever has been discovered of the perpetrators of the numerous robberies.

(The Argus, 30 May 1891)

ATTEMPTED SUICIDE: IN FRONT OF A LOOKING-GLASS

Yesterday at about noon Bridget Ryan, wife of Daniel Ryan, a labourer, residing at 49 Wilson-street, Brunswick, attempted to end her life by cutting her throat. At the time she was alone in the house, her husband being away attending St. Ambrose's Roman Catholic Church, Brunswick. In the midst of the service he was summoned home by a messenger, who informed him that his wife was dying.

He hurried home and found that his wife had very nearly succeeded in an endeavour to commit suicide. Her throat was horribly gashed, and Dr Talbot, who was immediately sent for, considered her condition so dangerous that he ordered her removal to the Melbourne Hospital. The police saw the doctor's directions carried out, and the woman since her admission to the hospital has progressed satisfactorily.

The manner in which Mrs. Ryan tried to accomplish her death was exceedingly strange. It appears that, having conceived the mad determination, she selected three of the sharpest of the table knives in the house, carried them into her bedroom, and placed them on the dressing-table. Then, standing in front of the looking-glass, she commenced her task. Before she had finished it she screamed and alarmed a neighbour, who, rushing into the house, discovered the woman lying upon the floor.

The neighbour's arrival was most opportune, for besides preventing her from continuing to hack at her throat as she might have done, it secured prompt medical attendance. Mrs Ryan's motive for self-destruction is unknown, but her husband says she has been drinking latterly, and presumes that her rashness was due to the effects of drink.

(The Argus, 29 June 1891)

LARRIKINISM AT BRUNSWICK

The Brunswick Town Council, owing to the repeated complaint made of the numbers of young men collecting and loitering about the corners of the main Sydney-road, recently passed a by-law for the removal of the nuisance, and issued instructions to the police to enforce the by-law, with the result that at the Brunswick Court yesterday a batch of young men were brought before the Bench charged with loitering about the street corners on the 28th ult. The nuisance caused by these persons has become a great annoyance, especially to ladies, as, owing to their numbers, pedestrians are jostled into the gutters. Fines varying from 10s. to 20s. were inflicted in each case.

(The Argus, 9 July 1891)

SUICIDE AT WEST BRUNSWICK: A DAIRYMAN ALMOST CUTS HIS HEAD OFF

A dairyman named William Palmer, residing at West Brunswick, committed suicide yesterday by cutting his throat in a horrible manner. Owing, it is said, to matrimonial infelicity, Palmer, who is 55 years of age, and is well known and much respected in his neighbourhood, was yesterday much depressed in mind, and immediately after dinner, which was at 2 o'clock, went to his room and remained apart from the family until 6 o'clock.

At that hour one of his daughters went to tell him that tea was ready, and, not finding him in his room, sought him in the premises attached to the house, and found him lying in a shed with his throat gashed so terribly that his head was almost severed from his body. By his side was found a table-knife all blood-stained, and it was evident from this and from the further fact that the body was cold, that the man must have gone straightway from the dinner table to his room and thence to the shed and ended his life in the fashion described.

The police were communicated with, and they made arrangements for the care of the body, pending the inquest. Palmer, who was in fairly comfortable circumstances, leaves a wife and two children.

(The Argus, 27 July 1891)

POLICE NEWS: RIDING OVER A CHINESE

Ah Fong sued George McIntyre. Mr Phillips for plaintiff and Mr. Grylls for defendant.

The facts were that on the 16th of June, McIntyre deliberately rode over the Chinese whilst the latter was walking along the footpath in Nicholson-street, East Brunswick. Ah Fong gave evidence to prove the assault complained of. He was walking in the same direction as the horse was going, and did not see it coming. Two boys who were near shouted to him, but it was too late to get out of the way.

John Atchinson, a driver in the employ of Ford Bros., stated that he had seen McIntyre ride over the Chinaman. Constable Dyson gave evidence as to Ah Fong giving information to him of the occurrence, and his subsequent tracing.

Mr Grylls contended that the act was not done wilfully. Defendant was fined 20s., with £2 2s. costs.

(The Coburg Leader, 29 July 1891)

A BRUNSWICK BRUISER

James Hegarty, of police court fame, appeared at the Brunswick court on Wednesday in the character of a prosecutor. He charged a man named Miller with threatening his life, and it appeared that Hegarty had taken Miller in out of charity (so Hegarty said), and fed him so well that Miller waxed strong and kicked. That is he used to throw himself into fighting attitudes of an evening, and wrestle with the wall. On these occasions he flung his arms so wildly about that Hegarty "trembled yer Worships" with fear. This J. L. Sullivan [*first heavyweight boxing champion of the modern era*] business developed until Miller wanted to make a punching bag of his hosts head, and when the latter objected the guest went for the wood axe to make mince meat of Hegarty.

This aggrieved individual informed the Bench that he did not expect such conduct from the defendant, because "he went down on his knees every night and said his prayers."

The joke in this case is that Miller is a feeble old man, short sighted and deaf. His teeth have long since departed, and it is as much as he can do to wrestle with a loaf of crusty bread, much less frighten old and experienced individuals with muscular exhibitions. The ferocious nature of the defendant was so little understood by the Bench that they dismissed the case.

(The Coburg Leader, 29 July 1891)

THE BRUNSWICK FATALITY: THE INQUEST

The district coroner, Mr. Candler, held an inquest on Saturday at the Grandview Hotel, West Brunswick, touching the death of the man Charles Andrews, who was killed by an explosion at the Hoffman Brick Company's works on Friday...

Edward Hickey, the foreman of the works, in endeavouring to account to the jury for the premature explosion, said he could not give any feasible explanation of it, but thought it might have occurred through a match dropping into the hole out of Andrews's pockets. He was a smoker, and the men would smoke at their work in defiance of the regulations which forbade them doing so.

The coroner having summed up, the jury returned a verdict of "accidental death."

(The Argus, 14 September 1891)

BRUNSWICK BOARD OF ADVICE

The Brunswick Board of Advice met last Tuesday evening in the Albert-street State School...

A complaint of cruelty against Mr. Watson was then heard. The Mother of a boy named Charles Derham said her son had played truant for some time, and when found out his father had locked him up, given him bread and water, and thrashed him. On a Wednesday she took him to school, and told Mr. Watson about the punishment the boy had received, and asked him not to inflict any more. He promised he would not, but as soon as she went away Watson took the boy upstairs and caned him so severely that blisters were raised on his hands. The boy then ran out of the school and went home.

He was frightened to go to it, and she had to send him to Mr. Hayden's school. She had since been summoned for not having the boy at school the required number of days. After a patient hearing the Board considered that the charge of cruelty could not be proved.

(The Coburg Leader, 14 October 1891)

FIRES AT BRUNSWICK

Shortly after 1 o'clock yesterday morning a night watchman, employed in the vicinity of the Cumberland Arms Hotel, Sydney-road, Brunswick, discovered that a fire had broken out in a fruit shop at the corner of Martins-lane and Sydney-road. He alarmed Foreman F. J. Batt, of the Brunswick branch of the Metropolitan Fire Brigade and the firemen were soon zealously engaged in the task of subduing the flames. Though they succeeded in doing it inside half an hour the fruit shop was totally destroyed, and the adjoining building, also a fruit shop, was severely damaged...

Before the firemen had completed their labours on the Sydney-road they were called to the works of the Willsmore Brick Company where the oil-house, in which were stored about 20 barrels of oil, was found to be in flames. The fire was quickly mastered, eight barrels of oil only being sacrificed. The origin of this fire is a mystery.

(The Argus, 20 October 1891)

ROBBERY AT BRUNSWICK

A daring robbery was committed at the Edinburgh Castle Hotel, corner of Albion-street and Sydney-road, Brunswick, between 9 and 10 o'clock on Friday night. Soon after the latter hour Mrs. Summers, wife of the licensee, found a skeleton-key in the door of an upstairs room, and on making a close inspection of the room discovered that £14 10s. 9d. in silver and £16 odd in notes and gold had been stolen. Two suspicious-looking characters were observed in the bar of the hotel at about 9 o'clock, and it is concluded that one kept the licensee and his wife in conversation while the other committed the robbery. The police are searching for the men referred to.

(The Argus, 27 October 1891)

THE BLIGHTED BRUNSWICK BOBBY

We met him on Sydney-road a few days ago, and he seemed a sadly changed man. The springy step, joyous look, and ringing laugh of former days had gone, and a weary, hunted expression shone out of his furtive eyes. He carried a much thumbed book under his arm, which he now and again earnestly studied, and it was during one of these mental exercises that we accosted him.

"Well Wilcox! How are you getting along with the vaccination notices?"

He lifted his head slowly and looked sadly at us in a reproachful manner, and then in accents full of emotion he answered, "How can you ask me such a question. Are you not doing your best to make my life miserable. You are writing articles in the papers, calling on the people not to poison their children with diseased vaccine matter, and everywhere I go, Andrade* is ahead of me with a handbill, urging parents on no pretence to vaccinate their innocent offspring. I get more abuse in a day than Graham Berry* got in ten years, and I have to bear it, for my abusers are women."

"What do they call you?" we broke in.

"Almost everything. One woman said I was a 'Pandorian Plague Cart' and ought to be shot into Kettle's quarry."

"She must have got that phrase from Dr. Talbot*," we interrupted. "And considering that Sergeant Brown selected you for the duty, because you are the handsomest man in the local force, it's rather hard to be abused by the ladies like that."

"Yes. If they threw a brick at me I could dodge it, but when half a dozen mothers assemble when they see me coming, and start a vocal fusillade, it's terribly irritating. I can stand a good deal, but this work is breaking me down. I suppose you notice the difference in me. I feel ten years older than I did a month ago. But I must be going now. I have 120 notices to serve today, and if anything happens give me credit at any rate for having perished doing my duty."

He shook hands in a mournful way. And as we watched his bent and weary figure go down a side street, with the well thumbed book opened before him, we too turned sadly away with a sigh, as we thought of the grievous blight that had thus suddenly fallen on this hitherto joyous life.

*Presumably David Andrade, founder of the Melbourne Anarchist Club and a newsagent at 729 Sydney Road, North Brunswick

* Graham Berry, Victorian Premier and Treasurer 1875-81

*Dr. Talbot, Health Officer, used the phrase 'Pandorian plague cart' at a meeting of the Brunswick Public Works committee in October 1891

(The Coburg Leader, 2 December 1891)

SERIOUS AFFRAY IN BRUNSWICK

Yesterday afternoon, at half-past 4 o'clock, a free fight took place amongst a number of stonebreakers and carters in Dawson-street, West Brunswick, resulting in serious injury to one of them. A number of men are employed in making the street in question, and on a vacant piece of land close by about a score of stonebreakers are at work.

Yesterday a number of these were keeping up the Christmas festivities, and a quantity of beer was drunk, which led to a quarrel. A carter named Alexander Gaffyn, who resides in Barkly-street, was at work in the place, and he became involved in a free fight which resulted.

The broken metal was used as missiles, and a piece of bluestone nearly 3lb. in weight struck Gaffyn on the back of the head, laying the skull bare. The man was partly stunned, and was brought to Dr. Hamilton, who found that, in addition to the severe flesh wound, there was also concussion. The wounded man was so dazed with the blow that he is unable to say who threw the stone at him. The police have the matter in hand.

(The Argus, 29 December 1891)

A HOUSEBREAKER ARRESTED: DESPERATE STRUGGLE

Housebreaking in the suburbs has been increasingly prevalent of late, and, owing to householders leaving their houses unprotected, the thieves are usually able to effect the robbery with little chance of detection. Late yesterday afternoon, however, two housebreakers were caught in the act, and though one of them succeeded in making his escape, the second was captured after a hard struggle in which he severely injured one of the rangers of the Royal-park by blows from a hammer-headed whip.

The house at which the robbery was committed is situated in Brunswick-road, Brunswick, and is occupied by a Mr. Blyth, who, with his family, is supposed to have left Melbourne for a short holiday. At about 4 o'clock in the afternoon a girl saw two men trying the front door of the house with keys, and finally, as they could not effect an entrance, they went round to the back of the house and broke in through a window. The girl gave the alarm to a Mr. McFarland, but before he could reach the house the two men came out and took to their heels, through the park.

They were pursued on horseback by the park ranger, Mr. Maker, who came up with one of the thieves after a chase of about a mile. Tho man, who was armed with a hammer-headed stockwhip, turned savagely on Mr. Maker, and struck him several times about the head, but the ranger, though badly bruised, stuck to his man until Constables Black and Murphy, of the Royal-park police station, came up, and the man was handcuffed. During the chase he was seen to throw away a bunch of skeleton keys, and these having been picked up, the prisoner was taken to the Royal-park watchhouse, where he gave his name as Edward Chanmare, a carpenter, 23 years of age.

He will be presented before the local Bench today charged with housebreaking, with having housebreaking implements in his possession, and with assault. The second man has not yet been arrested. Owing to Mr. Blyth's absence the value of the property stolen has not been ascertained.

(The Argus, 12 January 1892)

AFFRAY WITH LARRIKINS

A number of Collingwood larrikins created a disturbance at Brunswick on Saturday afternoon, which terminated by their committing a savage assault upon Constable Seddon at Brunswick, resulting in such severe injuries that medical skill had to be obtained to attend to his injuries.

At about 3 o'clock a cab load of young men called at Fraser's Moreland Hotel and ordered drinks which after consuming they refused to pay for. They drove in the direction of Coburg, Mr. Fraser followed them to the Coburg Cricket-ground where the Capulet Club from Collingwood were playing, they were there identified, and after considerable trouble subsequently paid for their drinks. As it was feared that they would again visit the hotel on their return, Constable Seddon was instructed to be in readiness near the place. At about 5 o'clock they returned from Coburg, but passed the hotel, contenting themselves with yelling and swearing as they passed. Seddon, who was in the vicinity, hearing the row, went towards the cab when disgusting language was used towards him. He followed the cab, and jumped on to the step to remonstrate with them, when one of the young men struck him on the face; the blows were repeated several times and when opposite the police station another of the men hit the constable such a severe blow as to knock him off the step on to the road.

The action overbalanced his assailant who fell also out of the cab on to the street. The vehicle stopped when the others in the cab, four in number, attacked Seddon while on the ground, kicking him savagely. A civilian named Samuel Reeves pluckily came to the assistance of Seddon, and he was also illtreated, being kicked on the legs. Two of the men were eventually overpowered and handcuffed and rushed to the lock-up, which was only one hundred yards away. The others succeeded in effecting their escape.

The men gave their names as Edward Pollykett and James Elton, and their residence as Collingwood. But for the timely arrival of Reeves the constable would have been much more seriously hurt. His injuries are very severe, his head being very much cut, his legs black, and the worst injury being on the mouth, which is badly smashed from a kick, two of his teeth being missing. Dr. Hamilton had to be sent for and attended to Seddon's wounds. The men will be brought before the court at the next sitting.

(The Argus, 15 February 1892)

FATAL ACCIDENT AT BRUNSWICK

Alfred Thomas Sanderson, 20 years of age, who resided at 42 Hope-street, Brunswick, and was employed by Messrs. Ford Brothers, bakers, died at his residence yesterday from injuries sustained on the 15th inst. by a fall from a cart. Sanderson drove a delivery-cart, and whilst getting into it the horse started off before he had taken a seat, and he was thrown heavily to the ground upon his head. He was removed to his home, and attended to by Dr. Stewart, but his injury, a fracture of the skull, was so serious that he sank and died yesterday. An inquest will be held at the Courthouse Hotel, Brunswick, at 11 o'clock this morning, by Dr. Neild, the acting district coroner.

(The Argus, 20 February 1892)

INQUEST

An inquest was held by Dr Neild at the Sadowa Hotel, Brunswick, on Saturday, on the body of a boy named John Frederick Judge, aged 12 years, who was drowned the previous afternoon by falling into a clayhole at the corner of Edward and Charles streets, Brunswick. Evidence was given by a companion of the deceased named Spurring that they were running round the hole, and that the deceased tripped and fell into the water. A verdict of accidental drowning was returned by the jury.

(The Argus, 7 March 1892)

SERIOUS ACCIDENT AT BRUNSWICK

About half-past nine on Sunday night a painful accident happened opposite the tram sheds, North Brunswick, to a celestial named Ah Koon, 23 years of age, who is in the employ of Ah Suey, Manning-street, Coburg.

It appears about the above time mentioned, Ah Koon was on a tramcar coming from Melbourne, and when near the terminus he attempted to jump off, while the car was in motion, and in doing so, he slipped and fell heavily on the wooden blocks. When picked up and carried into the tram shed, he was found to be unconscious, and to have received a severe cut and wound, which bled profusely.

He was at once taken to the Melbourne Hospital, where he was admitted by Dr. Cook and in addition to the scalp wound he was found to be suffering from concussion of the brain. Had it not been for the promptness of the gripman in bringing the car to a standstill, no doubt a fatal accident would have resulted.

(The Coburg Leader, 23 March 1892)

DYNAMITE OUTRAGE AT BRUNSWICK: MAD DEED OF AN ECCENTRIC WOMAN: ATTEMPTED MURDER AND SUICIDE: A SENSATIONAL STORY

An extraordinary deed of violence was committed in one of the quietest parts of Brunswick early yesterday morning. It was manifestly intended to cause the loss of at least two lives, and was carried out with considerable cunning and skill, but it fortunately failed to accomplish all that was hoped. In place of the two fatalities there has so far been no loss of life. The locality of the crime is a short thoroughfare named Walter-street, running north of Albion-street west. In Walter-street there are four houses, three of weatherboard and one of brick, which are concerned in yesterday's outrage. The brick house is occupied by a Mr. Sisson and the three others by Mrs. Ryckman, a widow, Mr. and Mrs. Chatfield, and Mr. and Mrs. O'Halloran.

The widow Ryckman – Mary Ann Elizabeth Ryckman – went to reside in the first of the three weatherboard cottages about four or five years ago. She was understood at the time to be only recently widowed and she and her little boy were consequently the objects of much neighbourly sympathy until by her repellent manner she forced those around her to leave her alone. Two years ago the Chatfields, a young married couple, moved into the house adjoining that occupied by Mrs. Ryckman, and very speedily neighbourly and kindly relations were set up and as speedily broken again, partly because of a quarrel between Mrs. Ryckman's boy Albert and an adopted son of the Chatfields.

Day after day the friction between the widow and Mrs. Chatfield was demonstrated openly and in the usual fashion until at last it became a quarrel which brought out the worst side of Mrs. Ryckman's eccentric character, and showed her to be a woman who, when driven by passion, would not stop short of violence. At first she appeared desirous of escaping from the neighbourhood, and having handed her boy over to the care of Mr. Barbour, of the Gordon Institute, tried to sell her house, which she had acquired or was acquiring through the medium of one of the building societies. After sending her son away she devoted herself to her trade – that of a tailoress. This gave her plenty of occupation for her thoughts, but her loneliness in the absence of her son preyed so much on her mind that her eccentricities, which were for a while held well in check, exhibited themselves more markedly than before, and Mr. and Mrs. Chatfield at last determined that as Mrs. Ryckman could not leave they would do so. They found themselves in a difficulty, just as Mrs. Ryckman had done. They were buying their house through a building society, and being unable to sell their acquired rights owing to the depression, had either to forfeit all they had paid or remain where they were.

Two months ago, and often before and since, Mrs. Ryckman went to the North Brunswick police station and complained of the ill-treatment and insults which she said were put upon her by Mrs. Chatfield. A constable visited the house upon the particular occasion referred to as being two months ago, and while he was inside listening to the woman's complaint a large piece of wood was thrown upon the roof. This of itself, though trifling, was accepted by the police as an evidence of the ill-will and mischievous bent of some of Mrs. Ryckman's neighbours, and though no court proceedings were ever initiated by Mrs. Ryckman, a word of caution was given that it would be as well, as the woman was eccentric, to let her severely alone.

The next prominent incident in the squabble shows Mrs. Ryckman to have been unmistakably aggressive. Mrs. Chatfield had grown utterly weary of the trouble, and had begun to fear that her ill-natured neighbour might do her some violent injury, as she had often threatened. She therefore determined to go away for a few days to see whether that would be beneficial, intending if it did not to leave the locality permanently, even should it become necessary to sacrifice the house. Accordingly on the afternoon of Wednesday last she was walking towards the house of Mrs. O'Halloran to ask her to look after her house for a few days, when Mrs. Ryckman, she says, struck her in the face with some branches of garden shrubs, and reviled her in obscene and passionate language. Mrs. Chatfield replied mildly, but sarcastically, and the widow retorted, and struck her a heavy blow on the face. After this incident Mrs. Chatfield having taken out a summons against Mrs. Ryckman for assault, went on a visit to her mother-in-law, at Mercy-street, South Yarra.

The summons was to have been heard at the Brunswick Court to-day, and it would seem that this fact so disturbed Mrs Ryckman that she determined to end her own life and that of the Chatfields on the day before. Late on Monday night she was seen by Mrs. O'Halloran standing upon Chatfield's verandah, but not more than passing notice was taken of the fact at the time. Mrs. Chatfield was still away at South Yarra, and Mr. Chatfield had not returned for the night. When he did return he ate some supper and went to bed, and soon fell asleep. Mrs. Ryckman must have been watching him the whole time through the windows, for at about half-past 1 o'clock, not long after he went to sleep, he was awakened by a noise, and looking towards the door of his room saw a bright light, and behind it the face of Mrs. Ryckman. He sprang out of bed to extinguish the light, but before he could reach it there was the sound of a loud explosion and he was knocked down, bruised, cut, and bleeding, and was instantly unconscious. The noise of the explosion was so great that it awakened not only the immediate neighbours, but many others for a considerable distance round, and sent them hurrying to the place to find out what had happened.

Senior-Constable Jackson and Constable Jolly were quickly on the spot, and, having extricated Chatfield from the timbers of the house that encumbered him, and from which, in his weak and exhausted condition, he could not free himself though he had recovered his consciousness, they summoned Dr. Overend, who gave him careful attention. The neighbours by this time suspected that the explosion had been the work of Mrs. Ryckman, and they told the police so. Jackson and Jolly knew enough of the relations existing between the Chatfields and Mrs. Ryckman to know that the suspicion was a justifiable one, and they therefore went to her house to question, and if necessary, to arrest her. But they recognised the necessity of being cautious, and of taking every precaution lest they might be made victims too. They went quietly to the woman's house, and finding both doors locked agreed to force an entrance, the one at the back and the other at the front, simultaneously. As Jolly was passing the side window on his way to the rear he was thrown backwards by the rush of air and flying glass from the window, and was thus forcibly and unpleasantly made aware of a second explosion, this time in the house of Mrs. Ryckman. Fortunately, Jolly escaped without injury, and being joined by Jackson both got into the house, and came upon Mrs. Ryckman sitting in a chair by her bedside bathing her arm, which was horribly shattered and bleeding fast.

She said little, though she acknowledged that it was she who had perpetrated the outrage at the Chatfields house. She and Chatfield were removed to the Melbourne Hospital as speedily as was possible, and were there attended to by Dr. Crowley. Chatfield was in great pain, and appeared to be dangerously wounded. His face and body are badly burned, and his eyelashes and much of his hair are singed off. His right leg is dreadfully burned, the bone below the knee being almost charred. Altogether his condition is serious, and the shock to his system so severe that in addition to the amputation of his leg, which is almost certain to become necessary, he may suffer still more grievously, and may not recover.

The woman's left arm was mutilated horribly, the hand being blown completely off above the wrist. The other arm and portions of her body are badly burned, but her condition generally is such that she may be expected to recover. The house shows how nearly successful was Mrs. Ryckman's attempt to take life. There are three rooms, the front being used for a sittingroom, the centre one for a bedroom, and the last for a kitchen. A passage runs along the whole length of the house, and it was in the passage beside the bedroom door that the explosion occurred. Here a hole nearly a foot square has been made in the flooring boards, and round and about this hole is a heap of wreckage consisting of furniture and fittings and portions of the house itself. The dividing wall is shattered, the ceiling broken in places, the side wall shifted out of plumb and detached from the roofing, the window glass smashed, and the pictures, ornaments, and nick-nacks generally in the bedroom and kitchen strewn in pieces all over the floors. Looking at the house it must certainly be considered that, severe as Chatfield's injuries undoubtedly are, he escaped lightly compared with what his fate might have been.

Mrs. Ryckman's house escaped the serious damage suffered by Chatfield's, because of the different positions in which the explosive was placed. In Chatfield's house it was put upon the floor in the passage, and striking downwards, as is its natural tendency, it met the resistance of the boards, which caused it to expand and do widespread mischief. In the other case Mrs. Ryckman placed it upon her bed or held it in her hand while she set it alight, and having blown off her hand it expended its force in the soft flock mattresses upon the bed, and went no further, save that the panes of glass in the window of the room were shattered.

Reading in the light of what may be gathered from statements of the principals and from an inspection of the houses the story of the antecedents of the outrage, and of the outrage itself, is a pathetic one. Mrs. Ryckman, who is about 35 or 40 years of age, was widowed, it is said, by the wreck of the *Dandenong*, and the tragic death of her husband threw her upon the world, and to a modified extent unhinged her mind. Her struggle to maintain herself and her boy, of whom she is passionately fond, accentuated her eccentricities and embittered her mind, and, in addition to growing particularly sensitive, she became violent whenever the happiness of her little lad appeared to be jeopardised. These traits account for much of the trouble with Mrs. Chatfield, and the police are disposed to think that her action on Monday morning is to be ascribed more to her mental state than to any malice or criminality on her part. She developed a dislike to Mrs. Chatfield because she thought that in some way her boy had been injured, and the quarrelling that followed was the ordinary result of such bickering.

At last she made provision for the future of her boy and determined to end her life and avenge herself upon her neighbours at the same time. With this purpose in her mind she secured some plugs of Nobel's lithofracteur, and having watched all night for Mr. Chatfield's return, selected a favourable moment when he had gone to bed, and having slipped into the house by some means at present unknown, she placed the explosive and a lighted piece of fuse attached beside the bedroom door, and, satisfied that nothing could save her enemy, escaped out of the building before the explosion. She hurriedly ran to her own house and locked herself in. Then she sat down on her bed with the open summons before her, and more dynamite plugs within her reach. When the noise outside told of the arrival of the neighbours and the police she took the dynamite and, applying a match to it, held it in front of her. She apparently did not understand the nature of the explosive thoroughly, for by holding it as she did she merely succeeded in shattering her hand.

The unfortunate woman tells her own story in two letters addressed to Mr. Barbour, of the Gordon Institute, which were found in her pocket. The letters run as follow:

"25|4|92.

Edward-cottage, Walter-street, Albion-street W., Brunswick.

Mr. Barber,

Sir, - Please, for dear Rickter's sake, do with everything what you think best; sell or let the cottage. There is £50 15s. to pay yet for it; there is £13 3s. to pay for two blocks of land in Millar-street, Upper Yarraville; there is 18s. rates due for the cottage; there is £1 8s. due for rates in Agness-street, Yarraville; there is no other money to pay anywhere or for anything; there is in my purse 16s., and no doubt you will have the things all sold. There will then be enough to pay for my burial. There need be no fuss over me with doctors, as I do it myseph rather than live the life I get from the woman next door to me. She is constantly calling me a pickpocket and other filthy names, and also throwing over muck every day almost, that I find there is no stoping her, as she says I cannot do her any harm, as I have no witness. I have advertised seven times, but only got one answer and that a person I should not like in my place so rather than live in misery I will die. Please be kind to poor Bertie, as he is now all alone. I would rather he did not know how I die if you can help It. Hoping you will forgive me troubling you so much, I remain one worried to deth,

    M. A. E. RYCKMAN

    2|5|92.

    P.S. Since I wrote the above I tried to live on, but on Wednesday, 27th, when I was cutting down the flowers in the front, she came pass and called me a pickpocket, and so I thought of what was rong, and slaped her face. Then she fell down. I told her she could go, as I would not fear her any more, as I found she could not do what she has threatened me so often, but she has taken out a summons for me to go to court. I have put up with for over 12 months to keep out of court, and after all it is come to this. But rather than let her have her way for so long and then be compelled to go where she sayes she would make me go, I will try another way, I cannot help it. She has done so much. It is her that has made me and my child part, so she did not like me to interfere with her once."

    The other letter reads:

    "25|4|02.

    "Edward-cottage, Walter-street, off Albion-street, Brunswick.

    Mr. Barber,

    Dear Sir, - Please for Bertie's sake do with everything for the best. Sell or let the cottage, which you think best. There is £50 15s. to pay the cottage. There is £13 Ss. to pay, for two blocks of land in Millar-street, Upper Yarraville. My deeds and all papers are in a tin box in the large box on the verandah. Please do take care of poor Albert, as he has no one in this world to if you do not – do not let him know what I have done if you can; and if there is any nice Elderly lady and gentleman who would like him as their own, then let them have him, so he can take their name. I put up so long with the woman next door to me that life is a Burden to live beside her, and I cannot get away. I have tried hard, very hard. She will not let me pass in or out, nor will she pass any time without calling me bad names or throwing dirt over. There is no stoping. I fe---"

(The Argus, 4 May 1892)

KILLING A HORSE

A poor equine wreck made up its mind to die, and in its simplicity laid down on a footpath near the Brunswick Police Station. As its poor tired spirit was about to take its departure to the "happy pasture grounds," a constable came up, bringing the police armoury with him, and placing the revolver to its head, shut his eyes and fired.

When the smoke cleared away, the horse looked reproachfully at the constable, who again fired at him. This evidently did the horse good, for he got up and walked across the road. The constable was shocked at this contemptuous treatment of his marksmanship, and catching sight of a sardonic grin on the horse's features, fired at its tail without injuring that useful appendage.

This was too much for both, and after a scrimmage the constable got the nag's head "in chancery," and only after its weight had been increased by three pounds of lead, would the horse die. If it had been allowed to adhere to its original intention, it would have succumbed in a few minutes after lying down. It is very evident that the use of dynamite is the only sure way of killing a horse within an hour.

(The Coburg Leader, 3 August 1892)

THE BRUNSWICK DYNAMITE OUTRAGE: TRIAL OF MRS RYCKMAN: ACQUITTED ON THE GROUND OF INSANITY

Mary Ann Ryckman, a widow, aged about 32, was placed on her trial yesterday at the criminal sittings at the Supreme Court, before Mr Justice Holroyd, on the charge of unlawfully and maliciously damaging property by using a certain explosive whereby the life of Charles Edwin Chatfield, a printer, was endangered.

Mr Finlayson prosecuted for the Crown, and Sir Bryan O'Loghlen, Q. C., defended the prisoner.

The case for the prosecution was that Mr. Chatfield lived in a cottage in Walter-street, Brunswick, in May last, and the prisoner resided in another cottage built on the allotment of land adjoining that on which Chatfield's cottage was erected. The prisoner had no occupation, and had one child, and owned the property on which she lived. For some considerable time before May last Mrs. Chatfield and Mrs. Ryckman had been on exceptionally bad terms with each other. Mrs. Chatfield's account of affairs was that she never gave the prisoner any occasion for being on bad terms with her, but according to a letter and documents found in the prisoner's house after the explosion it was certain that she believed that Mrs. Chatfield had treated her in a very bad way, by calling her foul names and throwing garbage and old boots and other things into her yard.

On the 27th April last, matters were brought nearer to a culmination by an alleged assault by the prisoner on Mrs. Chatfield. The latter took out a summons against the prisoner for assault, and she was to appear on the summons at the local police court on the 4th May. Mrs. Chatfield also considered it unsafe to live in her house any longer and went away to stay with a relative in another suburb. On the night of the 2nd May, Mr. Chatfield went to his home between 11 and 12 o'clock, and retired to bed about a quarter to 1 o'clock on the morning of Tuesday 3rd May. He fell asleep, and about half past 1 o'clock was aroused by a very loud explosion. He sprang out of bed, and seeing something on fire on the floor stamped on it and it immediately exploded, and inflicted on him fearful wounds.

His left leg was so much injured that he has not since been able to use it. His stomach was hurt, and also one of his eyes. He was taken to the Melbourne Hospital, and nine days after admission there the eye became so bad that he was removed to the Eye and Ear Hospital, where the eye had subsequently to be taken out. He was, in fact made into a complete wreck, and came into court yesterday on crutches.

After he jumped up in his house in consequence of the first explosion, he saw Mrs. Ryckman in the passage of it, and called out "You fiend what are you doing there?" She went away to her own house, and after some neighbours and other persons had collected in Chatfield's house an explosion was heard in the prisoner's house. They then went into her house and found that she had placed a piece of dynamite in her hand intending to put it in her mouth and kill herself, but it went off in her hand and blew it away and so injured the parts that her arm had afterwards to be amputated. There was no doubt that the prisoner had premeditated the outrage for a long time before she effected it, as the letter and documents found in her house showed that she intended to commit it on account of the ill usage which she considered she had received from Mrs. Chatfield. She had also purchased the dynamite somewhere for the purpose of using it as she did.

Dr. Overend, who saw the prisoner on the morning of the outrage, stated that he thought she was then suffering from melancholia and hallucinations. Such symptoms often led to suicide or homicidal mania.

Dr. Andrew Shields, chief Government medical officer, who was called, deposed that he had examined the prisoner. She was now rational. He had tried to ascertain the state of her mind about the time the outrage occurred, the 3rd May. It was six weeks ago since he first saw her, and he saw her practically every day after that. When she first went into the gaol she was peevish, and took offence at trifling things, but she improved, and was now rational. In his opinion the attempt of the prisoner to commit suicide was real and was not feigned. He thought she meant to take her own life and not that of Mr Chatfield; but merely to frighten or shock the latter.

Dr. Dick, superintendent of lunatic asylums, said he had examined the prisoner twice and he then thought she was sane. At the time of the explosion the prisoner was no doubt under the impression that she was being persecuted and labouring under delusions. If she attempted, under such a frame of mind, to commit suicide it would be doubtful whether she knew that she was doing wrong.

Sir Bryan O'Loghlen in defence of the prisoner said there was no doubt she had committed a crime, but the only question for the jury to consider was the state of her mind when she committed it. She was a person of extremely sensitive mind. Her boy had given her a great deal of trouble through running wild, and was placed under the charge of Mr. Barbour, of the Try Excelsior class, and her mind was no doubt seriously affected by the boy's conduct. In that state of mind she attributed to neighbours things that never occurred: but she believed thoroughly that they did. She thought one of her neighbours was dogging her and annoying her and considered herself persecuted in every possible way; but there was no doubt she was under delusions in that respect, and that she had lost control of her reasoning faculties at the time she committed the offence she was now charged with, and also when she attempted to commit suicide.

The jury after retiring for about 10 minutes, returned into court with a verdict of not guilty, on the ground that the prisoner was insane at the time she committed the act. HIS HONOUR ordered that the prisoner should be detained in gaol until the pleasure of the authorities respecting her was made known.

(The Argus, 30 August 1892)

ANOTHER ATTEMPTED OUTRAGE AT WEST BRUNSWICK

As a Mrs. McIntyre, a resident of Straw-street, West Brunswick, was walking home on Wednesday night last, she was met by a man about 30 years of age, who with the usual "mashing" remark, "Good evening, my dear" asked permission to see her home. This uncalled gallantry was declined, the lady telling her would-be admirer that she did not require an escort, and was well able to reach her domicile without his proffered company.

The gay Lothario would not take her rebuff, but persisted in following her, and when opposite a vacant piece of ground, he roughly seized the unprotected woman. Mrs. McIntyre screamed, and a person rushed to her assistance calling out, "Hello, what game are you up to here," and her cowardly assailant bolted.

Mrs. McIntyre at once proceeded to her sister's residence in Lyle-street for protection, and remained there for the night, and the following day reported the matter to Senior Constable Davidson, who anticipates making an arrest shortly.

(The Coburg Leader, 23 November 1892)

AN ABOMINABLE CHARGE

Charles H. Phillips aged 16, describing himself as a ropemaker was arrested by the Brunswick police on Thursday and charged with committing an abominable offence on a pretty mite of a girl named Lucy May Haines, only 7 years old. It is alleged that whilst Mrs. Haines, who resides in Tinning-street, Brunswick, was absent on Wednesday evening, the accused whose parents are neighbours, entered the house at about 9 o'clock and getting rid of Mrs. Haines little son by giving him a penny, gave the little girl a similar coin and then by his actions brought himself into his serious position. It is said that the accused admitted the offence. The doctors differ as to whether the substance of the charge, is correct. He will be brought before the Brunswick bench on Wednesday next.

(The Coburg Leader, 14 December 1892)

THE BRUNSWICK HEALTH OFFICER'S REPORT: POLLUTION OF MERRI AND MOONEE PONDS CREEKS

Dr. Talbot, the health officer of the town of Brunswick, has presented his annual report to the council. He states that taking into account the total absence of employment for working people, and the consequent privations to which they and their families are subjected, the health of the town for the past year has been satisfactory. In regard to the public schools, all the children appeared healthy and in good condition. The majority of dairies and milk-selling places (over 140 in the town) were in a passable condition.

Regarding the Chinese gardens, the officer says: - "Those gardeners are still day and night covering acres and acres of land with foul horse manure which has been collected from all parts of the town. In the interests of health no such gardens should be tolerated."

The report refers at length to the insanitary condition of the Moonee Ponds and Merri Creeks. Into the latter the drainage from a large Chinese piggery flows, as also the whole of the drainage of East Brunswick; and in addition nearly the whole of the drainage from the north and west of Northcote and of the tanneries and other works in Preston is brought into the creek down what is known as the Blind Creek. The matter brought down this creek is most offensive, and sometimes beyond description, and discolours the water of the Merri Creek while flowing past Brunswick.

Regarding the Moonee Ponds Creek, he mentions that hundreds of dairy cattle graze on the unfenced land on the west side of the town. Through this land the sewage flows into the Moonee Ponds Creek, and the cattle drink either this sewage or the water in the creek. Where the large drain ends at the entrance into the creek it is most offensive to the inhabitants and neighbourhood, and filter beds should be constructed.

During the year there were 858 births and 295 deaths in the town. There were 11 deaths from diphtheria and 26 from typhoid fever.

(The Argus, 25 February 1893)

BLASTING ACCIDENT: TWO MEN SERIOUSLY INJURED

Two men named Charles Macpherson, 30 years of age, who resides in Albert-street, East Brunswick, and Joseph Trafford, 23 years of age, of Victoria-street, Brunswick, were severely injured at a quarry off Nicholson-street, East Brunswick, yesterday morning. Whilst they were charging a hole with explosives, the charge prematurely exploded, and the blast struck the men about the face, hands, and arms, causing both very painful and serious injuries.

The comrades of the men removed them to the Melbourne Hospital with as much speed as was possible. Macpherson is progressing favourably, but Trafford is in a critical condition. As is not unusual with accidents of this class, the cause of the premature explosion is not known.

(The Argus, 15 March 1893)

A NICE LITTLE CARD PARTY

In company with his friend, William D'Arcy, Thomas Williamson entered on the 11[th] ult., the Grand View Hotel, West Brunswick, and just as they had finished their drinks,. Robert England asked him if he would make one in a little game of euc[h]re.

Quoth Williamson: "No thank you. I do not care to play with you. I've played once, but I will not do it again."

At this refusal, England, in company with his friends, sat down to their game of "cut throat" euchre. Williamson's curiosity overcame him, and he sauntered in and stood looking on at the game. England again endeavoured to persuade him to take a hand, but Williamson retorted that England had cheated by revoking. Fixing Williamson with his eye, England quietly sauntered up to him who on a sudden warbled, "He struck me without any warning."

England, in cross examination, said that since the days of his boyhood, he had never had a fight, and was so pleased with his first blow, which was a light one, that he put his whole heart into his blows, which he showed with cyclonic force around Williamson's square face, knocking out a tooth and raising sundry bumps on his forehead, calculated to puzzle a phrenologist. Witnesses corroborated this evidence. The defendant said he thought himself justified in thus forcibly resenting the indignity of being called a cheat.

After consideration the Bench inflicted a fine of £4 4s with £2 2s costs, in default, 14 days' imprisonment.

(The Coburg Leader, 29 March 1893)

ALLEVIATING THE DISTRESS OF BRUNSWICK

At the meeting of the Committee of the Brunswick Football Club, held on Monday evening last, it was unanimously decided that they should take steps for the holding of a fancy dress football match to take place on the 24th of May (Queen's Birthday) on the Brunswick Recreation Reserve, for the purpose of affording the much needed relief to the necessitous.

It is the intention of the club to write and ask the co-operation of the different societies and clubs in and around Brunswick, and to render all the assistance in their power to bring the object to a successful termination. A word of praise is due to the members of the club for the sympathy shown to their fellow townspeople who are in need of the common necessaries of life, and it is to be hoped that the residents of Brunswick will give the object their hearty support, and pay a small trifle at the gate, instead of jumping the fence as on subsequent occasions.

(The Coburg Leader, 15 April 1893)

SUNDAY LABOR AMONG CHINESE

At the last meeting of the Brunswick Town Council, a letter was received from Mr. Benjamin Binks, a resident of North Brunswick, complaining of the an[n]oyance he suffered though the working of chinese in their gardens on Sundays, and asking that the Council would endeavour to get the practice stopped. Cr. King made a somewhat impassioned speech on the subject, and declaimed against the wickedness of the chinese working in their gardens on Sundays and moved that the police be communicated with, and requested to enforce the bye-law.

Cr. Hatty seconded the motion, speaking also against the practises of Chinese in general, and their Sunday working in particular.

Cr. Hearn said he thought that the chinese were better employed in their gardens, than a lot of other people were who stood at street corners on Sundays, indulging in questionable language, and making themselves a general nuisance to passers by. But the motion was carried, despite this sensible protest.

It is really a question which will bear a good deal of looking at, as to whether these patient drudges are very great sinners in this action of theirs.

A wise old Roman said, "Labor is prayer," and Pauls says, "Be ye deligent in business." But the old Roman was only a pagan after all, and the apostle was probably not so holy as some of our latter day saints are. But it is probably wrong to work on Sundays.

Man and beast are better in having one days rest in seven. If they do not have it their health will be injured. But then comes the question what is rest? A man who works hard physically all the week, may fairly claim a right to lie on his back all Sunday, and rest the overtasked muscles, and one who sits at a desk pouring over the musty tomes, may find a refreshing health giving rest, in attending to his flower garden.

chinese, deligent, pouring etc all sic.
(The Coburg Leader, 15 April 1893)

FRIDAY'S TRAGIC OCCURRENCE: THREE CHILDREN DROWNED: A DISTRESSFUL SCENE.

It is with heartfelt regret that we have this week to chronicle one of the most pathetic occurrences that has taken place within our midst for many years, and Friday last, (Eight Hours' Day) will be a memorable one in the hearts of the afflicted parents of the three children, Emily Victoria Leary, aged 12 years; Catherine Alice, her sister, aged 8; and Wilhelmina Kennedy, aged 10.

Quite a gloom was cast over our town when it became known that the three innocent little children met their death by drowning between four and five o'clock on Friday afternoon, the 21st inst., in a disused clayhole, known as Firth's, by them venturing to have a sail on a frail raft. This raft is composed of three planks about 13 feet long, heavy nine inch planking, four inches thick and nailed together by three or four traverse pieces of soft wood, which would easily support the children.

The clayhole in which the fatality occurred is situated towards the south end of the brickyard, and is bounded on the south and west sides by houses which front Albert and Gardener streets, and on the north side it is some 40 or 50 yards from Victoria-street, which is unfenced, so that access to the hole is easy obtainable. The water in this spot is some nine or ten feet in depth, and runs east and west, so that some of the occupiers of the houses in Gardener-street can see the water from their back yard, which can be reached by a footway that runs to the surface of the water, some 70 or 80 feet below the level of the yard.

There are several of these clayholes in the vicinity, and on Friday last, about a dozen children went down to this fatal one, where the planks were floating about close to the water's edge, and three of the girls, Emily Victoria and Catherine Alice Leury and Wilhelmina Kennedy got upon it, intending to have a float about in the shallow water, but unfortunately the raft drifted out into the deeper part, when Wilhelmina Kennedy became frightened, and evidently not conscious of her risk, wanted to jump ashore, and in her nervousness would not wait for the raft to be pushed to the land, but prepared to jump over the two or three feet that separated her from the shore.

Her movements for this purpose causing the timbers to sway uneasily, she lost her balance, and in attempting to save herself she caught hold of Catherine Leury, and in a moment the two girls were in the water struggling with each other for support. The eldest of the three, Victoria Leury, was left alone on the plank, and seeing the other two come to the surface of the water, she, with distinguished bravery, gallantly jumped into the water to render assistance, at the same time giving a terrific scream.

A playmate of the children, Annie O'Connor, who saw the whole of the affair, began screaming at the top of her voice, and the noise attracted the attention of Mrs. O'Brien, whose back yard adjoins the hole, and as she was running down the embankment she looked into the water, where she saw the three children as they rose to the surface, making frantic efforts to catch hold of the raft, which had drifted away from them through the motions of the water caused by their struggling. As Mrs. O'Brien was climbing down the bank her foot slipped, and she fell and rolled some distance down the steep incline, which caused a few minutes delay, and when she arrived at the water's edge, she saw nothing but "bubbles."

In the midst of the wild rush for the water hole, and the shrieking, excitement and pitiful screams that prevailed, Mr. George Allen put in an appearance, and was one of the first men to respond to the cries for assistance. Mr. Allen, imagining to himself what had happened, began to throw off his outer garments as he proceeded to the water hole, and without any delay he bravely dived three times in succession, and on the last occasion he recovered the body of Catherine Leury, and handed her to some persons on the bank. Mr. Allen continued diving until he found himself almost exhausted, but his efforts to find the other bodies were fruitless, as it was impossible for him to see under the water, owing to its clayey colour.

As soon as the first body was recovered, misguided endeavours were made by some of the persons that had assembled, to restore the girl to consciousness, but without success. Shortly after Dr. Henry came on the scene, but his efforts were equally futile, and the child expired after an hour's labour attempting to restore animation.

The police were not long in securing drags, and recovered the last two bodies. By this time a large crowd had assembled round the great clayhole amongst whom was the fathers, James Kennedy and James Leury, and the mother of the victims, and as the bodies of the poor little children were being carried up to the top of the vast embankment, the scene was far beyond description, the screams and bitter tears that were shed was heart rending, and it was not without the aid of some kind neighbours that Mrs. Leury was taken to her home, where that day a deep and very dark cloud of sorrow rested.

(The Coburg Leader, 29 April 1893)

A DREADFUL DEN: HOW YOUNG PEOPLE ARE RECEIVED: THE MAXIMUM PENALTY IMPOSED

A case exhibiting some deplorable features was heard at the Brunswick Police Court on Wednesday last. The Town Council, through Senior-Constable Davidson, one of their Inspectors, proceeded against John Butler, of Barry-street, for having in his house on 12th May a dancing saloon, which he failed to register. The evidence showed that the place was frequented by young people of both sexes, and that the conduct carried on was very disgraceful.

The ordinary charge of admission was 6d., but on what was known as "late nights" the charge was increased to 1s. 6d., the fee being paid by the men and boys, the women and girls being admitted free. One young woman who was described as respectable complained of being treated roughly and spoken to obscenely because she refused to dance with a man who asked her. "Come on and go through this ----- dance," said the man, seizing her roughly by the arm. She objected, and was greeted with a torrent of obscenity which will not bear printing.

Another girl, who looked little more than a child, but who had a fortnight ago been convicted of vagrancy, and taken of by the Salvation Army, said in her evidence that she went to the place on the night of the 12th, and stayed there until past 3 a.m. on the morning of the 13th. That she then left with another girl, and she subsequently deposed to shocking depravity in which she and others had engaged.

Senior-Constable Davidson characterised the place as a regular den for the manufacture of prostitutes, and said that the language generally used was terrible. The bench fined Butler £20, with £5 5s. costs, or three months imprisonment. The man was fined £5 on a former occasion, or a month's imprisonment for the same offence, and the police say that some of his admirers made up the fine, but he took the money and went to gaol for the month.

(The Coburg Leader, 3 June 1893)

A PETITION FROM THE WOMEN OF BRUNSWICK

The cry of distress from unemployed men and suffering women and children, has penetrated the walls of Parliament, and if anything will spur Parliament to do something at once to alleviate the sufferings of the unfortunate people instead of squabbling over party questions, it is the piteous character of the appeals made to the humanity of members.

Sir Graham Berry brought before the House on Thursday last a petition from the distressed women of Brunswick, the list of which was as follows:

To the Honorable the speaker and to the Honorable Members of the Legislative Assembly, in Parliament assembled.

The petition of the undersigned women of Brunswick respectfully sheweth:

1. That many women and children are experiencing very hard times and are suffering keenly from want of food,

clothing, furniture, fuel &c.

2. That husbands[,] fathers, brothers cannot find employment.

3. That Bailiffs are very busy in our midst, that shelter of the best description is found for skins, fat, bones, wool and tallow, but ourselves and our children are quite overlooked in this respect in our so called Christian community.

4. That we think it is the first duty of the Government to provide for the necessary wants of a community and not to provide for one class and neglect the claims of another class.

5. That our district is poverty stricken and sickness is prevalent.

6. That there is plenty of land wants clearing and cultivating on which profitable employment for all able to work could be found, and happy homes could take the place of poverty and wretchedness.

We pray your Honorable House to forthwith enable our husbands, brothers and fathers to look after our health and comfort, and to provide for our little ones by making provision on the land or by assisting such as wish to get to West Australia, New Zealand or some other country. And your petitioners will ever pray, &c.

Signed by distressed women.

(The Coburg Leader, 8 July 1893)

PROCEEDINGS AGAINST A BRUNSWICK COUNCILLOR

The proceedings at the ordinary meeting of the Brunswick Town Council, which was held on Monday evening, proved very interesting to the ratepayers, about 300 of whom were in attendance. Cr. Talbot, the chairman of the Public Works Committee, reported that Cr. Fleming had been guilty of disorderly conduct at the meeting of the committee on the 10th inst., which, in consequence, had to be adjourned, as it was found impossible to proceed with the business owing to that Councillor's opposition.

Cr. King moved –

That this Council desires to express its regret and indignation at the disorderly conduct of Cr. Fleming at the meeting of the Public Works Committee held on the 10th inst., and instruct that a summons be taken out against him.

He said that the Council had been made the laughing stock of the colony by permitting one Councillor to obstruct all business. Cr. Fleming had every opportunity given him at the committee meetings for withdrawing and apologising, but he would not do it.

Cr. Allard seconded the motion.

Cr. Fleming said he had been treated like a dog and called by Cr. Allard a d----d puppy. (Laughter.)

Cr. Allard: Oh! Mr Mayor, is that true?

The Mayor: No; you never said anything of the kind.

Cr. Fleming (to the Mayor): You called me an infernal liar. Take care I don't take out a summons against you for trespass and damages. You sent a man on to land that is under my charge to work on it. You had no right to put that man [t]here. I am agent for the property.

After further discussion the Mayor put the motion, which was carried without dissent.

The meeting broke up at about 12.30, having been sitting from 7 o'clock.

(The Coburg Leader, 22 July 1893)

TRAFFIC IN BABIES: THE SHOCKING DISCOVERY AT BRUNSWICK: POSITIVE EVIDENCE OF MURDER: MRS. THWAITES ARRESTED AT SYDNEY: FULL PARTICULARS OF HER STRANGE CAREER: DIGGING OPERATIONS TO BE CONTINUED BY THE POLICE

The police did not continue their task yesterday of digging up the yards of the houses which had been occupied by the baby farmer Mrs. Thwaites. They had obtained in the three bodies found in the yards of the houses at Moreland-road and Davies-street, Brunswick, positive evidence of murder and there was therefore no urgent necessity for immediate resumption of the work of digging up the other yards in search of any other bodies which might have been buried there. It was more important that all attention should be paid to the work of tracing the movements of the woman so that she might be arrested quickly, and to that end Detectives Nixon, Cook, and Thompson, who were placed in charge of the case, directed their energy, and received the assistance of all sections of the police force.

In some respects their work was light, and easy of accomplishment. Details of the woman's life in Melbourne were rapidly obtained and they soon had a complete history of her movements from April last up till the date of her flight from the colony about the middle of the present month. Beyond that, however, they were confronted with difficulty, which threatened to make the arrest of the woman a matter to be only accomplished after much delay. Her disappearance was mysterious and complete, and she had not left a trace behind her as in all her other similar flights she had done.

However, the issue of the warrant for her arrest upon the charge of child abandonment in August was telegraphed to every colony, together with a description of her, and a request that special effort should be made to accomplish her arrest. To Sydney a special wire was sent, as it was confidently believed that she had gone there. When the telegrams had been despatched the detectives and police waited for the result of the *post-mortem* examination of bodies No. 2 and No. 3, which was being made by Dr. Neild.

The examination of body No. 1 was scarcely satisfactory, because, owing to the advanced stage of decomposition, it was almost impossible for the doctor to say with certainty whether or not the child had lived. Yesterday, however, the later-buried bodies were found to be capable of more satisfactory examination.

"No. 3" was the body of a female child which had lived for several days, and had then died from suffocation. "No. 2" was the body of a male child, and so much decomposed that it appeared unlikely that the cause of death would be discovered. However, upon close examination it was found that the child had lived for several months and that its death had been brought about by strangulation. There could be no doubt upon the point, because round its neck was a piece of cord about a foot long which had been tied tightly in a running knot. The knot had been pulled so tightly that the loop round the neck was little bigger than a half-crown piece. With this discovery Dr. Neild completed his task, and as soon as he had done so news of the finding of the cord was telephoned to the detective office, and Superintendent Kennedy attended at the office of Mr. Nicolson, P.M., and swore an information against Minnie Thwaites, *alias* Knorr, for the wilful murder of a male child, unknown, at Davies-street, Brunswick, during the months of April or May last.

While this was being done the Sydney police had been actively attending to the matter in their city, and a previous knowledge of the woman helped them to an early arrest. They discovered her in a house in Brisbane-street, where she had been residing with her husband, Rudolph Knorr, for about ten or twelve days. She had been delivered of a child on Monday, so it was impossible to place her in the watchhouse. However, a guard was placed over her and she will be handed over to the custody of the Melbourne police as soon as she has recovered sufficiently to be removed.

Now that the woman's arrest has been accomplished the digging up of the yards at houses she has occupied in the various suburbs of Melbourne will be resumed and continued until all have been thoroughly examined.

THE ARREST OF MRS. THWAITES: CHANCE RECOGNITION BY A CONSTABLE.
SYDNEY, WEDNESDAY.

The arrest of Millie, or Minnie Knorr, or Thwaites, was one of those lucky incidents which import elements of romance into the dry detail of police duty. Thwaites had been on the wanted list of the Sydney police in times past. Prior to 1888 she was a prominent figure in Sydney, being rendered conspicuous by constantly wearing a long ulster, which, however, did not conceal the lines of an extremely well-proportioned figure. She left after serving a term of imprisonment for misappropriating a sewing- machine. Since then the police had lost all sight of her until about a week ago, when a constable having occasion to go to a house in Brisbane-street was surprised to find the door opened by Mrs. Thwaites. He restrained his impulse to extend recognition to the woman, thinking then that the information he had gained might be of use to him at a future date. He little imagined that the *rencontre* would so soon be of service in a sensational case. When the Sydney authorities received word that Mrs. Knorr, *alias* Thwaites, was wanted in Victoria they had no difficulty in arresting her.

She alleges that she is married to Rudolph Knorr, who is now serving as a waiter in a restaurant in Pitt-street. The room they occupy is a rented apartment in a poor quarter of the city, and when the police entered the house to-day they found that two days previously Mrs. Thwaites had been confined of her fourth child. It was impossible under the circumstances to remove her, and therefore the detectives are now keeping the place under strict surveillance pending her recovery. It is probable that she may be remanded to the Benevolent Asylum, but no decision has yet been come to on this point.

The fact that Knorr and Mrs. Thwaites have only been in their present home for a week adds to the singularity of the chance which led to her identification. It seems that on Saturday night week the owner of the house saw the couple pass along the street, and then return and apply for accommodation, which was extended to them. A full view could be obtained of the premises from the street but neither Knorr nor his wife showed any desire to conceal themselves. At the time of their arrival they had no luggage, but they stated that they had come from Eastwood near Ryde. A day or two afterwards, however, a box bearing Melbourne labels was delivered for them at the house. When the detectives reached the place this morning Knorr was there, and he is stated to have displayed some slight agitation at their inquiries. He was detained and the police made their way up to Mrs. Thwaites's bedroom.

They questioned the woman, but she promptly denied any connection with the allegations made against her. At a later period in the day when directly charged with murder she made no specific denial, and admitted having lived in the houses mentioned, as well as having adopted children. Further than that she would not go. It is alleged that she has represented to the authorities that she is very well connected, and has asked that a certain clergyman in Sydney should be apprised of her arrest with a view to communicating with her people in England, and Knorr, who was removed to the lock-up, was released this afternoon, after having been detained for some little time.

LATER.

Knorr was questioned as to his movements of late, and admitted having recently resided near Melbourne with the woman previously referred to, who, he said, was his wife. He was detained at the police station for a time, but on receipt of certain instructions from Victoria the police permitted him to go about his business. To-morrow morning Mrs. Thwaites is to be transferred to the Benevolent Asylum. She is about 26 years of age. The house in Brisbane-street is occupied by a widow, who stated that when the woman became aware yesterday that the police were in the house she almost lost control over herself.

MRS. THWAITES'S CAREER IN MELBOURNE.

The particulars published yesterday showed that Mrs. Thwaites had been partial to shifting from house to house and from suburb to suburb, but the fuller information since obtained has shown that she was for months seldom longer than a few days in any particular house, and the little household furniture she burdened herself with was rarely out of the vans of the carrier. If this strange habit of hers was designed to conceal her identity, and prevent her full history becoming known later, it was not successful, because, in all her wanderings, she left behind her a trace as easily followed as a bush fire. This is illustrated by the facility and despatch with which the police arrived at a full and accurate record of her eccentric journeyings.

There is one point upon which, as yet, no definite information has been formed. It is the place of residence of the woman prior to her strange and fleeting occupancy of the single-fronted weatherboard villa on the flat near the Merri Merri Creek. The belief is that she had previously resided in Fitzroy or Carlton. There is good reason for this belief, as she appeared at the Fitzroy Police Court on the 7th March in the capacity of friend of a woman of ill-repute named Christina Gresham. This woman was charged with vagrancy and larceny of £1 from the person, and Mrs. Thwaites gave evidence on her behalf, in which she stated that she had visited Gresham often, had engaged her to do dressmaking, and believed her to be altogether incapable of the offence of larceny. The testimony of Mrs. Thwaites was given with much self-assurance, and had some weight with the magistrates, until the police upset it by their details of the life of the accused. A sentence of one month's imprisonment was imposed, and thenceforward the Fitzroy police were not brought into personal contact with the woman Thwaites, though they heard she was living at Princes-street, Carlton.

But while there is a doubt of her movements prior to April 10, there is none from that time forward. The statements of the nursegirls Harriet Drummond, Alice Clarke, and a third named Maud Taylor, as well as the investigations of Plain-clothes Constable Wilcox and other members of the police force, have shown conclusively that since April at least she has been engaged in baby-farming.

As is already known, she established herself at Moreland-road on April 10, and two days later engaged the services of the nursegirl, Harriet Drummond. On the same afternoon she borrowed the spade with which the hole in the back-yard was dug, and three days later she removed to the single-fronted brick building at 25 Davies-street, Brunswick. Two weeks afterwards the nursegirl Drummond was dispensed with, and, through the good offices of a baker's delivery man, the girl Alice Clarke was secured to fill the vacant situation. When the girl entered the house she found there Mrs. Thwaites and a child in long clothes known as "Gladys." This child was represented as the offspring of Mrs. Thwaites, who according to the girl Clarke and others appeared to be very fond of it, and paid considerable attention to it.

A week after the advent of Clarke a second child in long clothes was brought to the house, and its name was also "Gladys" – Gladys Creighton. Within a week this infant was removed by its aunt, and its removal only preceded its death by a short period. When the death was reported to the coroner the Clifton Hill police made representations which led to a searching investigation. In their opinion there were circumstances in the case which justified the gravest suspicion, and because of this belief they had given particular attention to the woman Thwaites whenever she visited Clifton Hill. One evening a constable "shadowed" her, because at the inquest she had been suspected of ill-treating or neglecting the child, and had refused to disclose her place of residence, or permit the mother or the aunt of the child to see it. They thus discovered that she lived at Davies-street. It is due to the woman to say that the jury acquitted her of all blame in connection with the death of this child.

During the stay at Davies-street she was joined by her husband. He had been represented as a mining manager at Broken Hill, and his absence from home was consequently not commented upon by the neighbours. The managership of the Broken Hill mine was, however, only a fiction, as the husband was really in gaol. With Mr. Thwaites's appearance the girl Clarke was asked if she would arrange to nurse the baby Gladys at home, "because Mr. and Mrs. Thwaites had much business of importance to do, and would be frequently absent from home in consequence." Mrs. Clarke was consulted, and as she had no objection the girl took the child to her home in Coburg, and for three weeks remained there.

When she returned she found that a child named Lily, three years of age, represented as a niece of Mr. Thwaites, had been added to the establishment. A little later a female child in long clothes was brought to the house by a Mrs. Sloane. It was seen by Clarke for a week only, when according to Mrs. Thwaites, it was returned to its mother. On or about the 20th of June the Davies-street house was deserted and the family removed to Kara Kara house, Jackson-street, St Kilda. At this house a second nursegirl appeared, one Maud Taylor, of Balaclava. She came in answer to an advertisement inserted in the paper for "a little girl to mind a baby." The two girls were soon initiated in their duties of administering milk and water and sugar to a community of babies which varied from two to nine or ten, but as a general average numbered half a dozen.

About a week after Kara Kara house was taken, Mrs. Josephs, a relative of the nursegirl Maud Taylor, was induced to take one of the children to nurse at a weekly fee, but when a few days later Thwaites went to her house with another baby and said he desired the girl to nurse the two of them at home Mrs. Josephs refused to have anything more to do with the children, and Thwaites had to take them back. As a result of this rebuff the girl was dismissed. The Thwaites remained at Kara Kara for a fortnight altogether, and during that time Mr. and Mrs. Thwaites were frequently absent from home all day and much of the night. The girls were therefore left in sole charge of the half-dozen children.

Alice Clark, who was 16 years of age, and five years senior to Maud Taylor, used to pass some of the dreary hours away reading the daily newspaper, and with a practised eye she scanned the advertising columns in which were notices calling for "kind persons to adopt children, &c." One day she noticed amongst these an advertisement which read –

"Mrs. Thwaites, please call on Mrs. Young. Anxious." The same day Mrs. Thwaites appeared to be upset, and one of the children, the girl Lily, was taken away. From Kara Kara the family removed to Sunbury cottage, near the Middle Brighton railway station. Here only one night was spent "because," as Mrs. Thwaites told the girl Clark, "the landlord said he could get more rent than she was willing to pay him."

Bayview-avenue, Auburn, was the next place they occupied, and here the name of Leegar, which had been assumed at Kara Kara, was dropped for that of "De Vere." Three days was the limit of their stay in their new home, because the owner of it was not enamoured of the appearance of the people when he called upon them. Mrs. "De Vere" appeared to be much disappointed at the owner's decision, because she liked the situation, and thought the house and furniture which she had agreed to hire for 12 months at the weekly rental of £1 6s. would suit her admirably.

From Auburn they removed to Malcolm-street, South Yarra, and under the name of "Florence" Mrs. Thwaites busied herself in bringing more children to the house in place of some which had been taken away. At Malcolm-street, Alice Clark (whose mother had learned something of the character of the Thwaites family) left their service, and when she returned a week later, for her clothes, she found that Mrs. Thwaites had disappeared, leaving Thwaites in charge.

From the point of the departure of the girl Clark there is no one who can speak of the household arrangements of the woman Thwaites. Plain-clothes Constable Wilcox, however, supplies the balance of the history as it was learned from inquiries which he made. He had followed the woman from house to house and from suburb to suburb, spurred on either by some unfortunate mother who had entrusted her child to Thwaites, or at the desire of people who had taken charge of a child from Mrs. Thwaites for a week, only to find later that they had been trapped into keeping it always or casting it on the state. Wilcox found her, and time after time settled the disputes which had arisen. But at last in July, when the Prahran Bench were troubled to know what to do with a number of these abandoned infants, she disappeared altogether. Wilcox traced her as far as Spencer-street railway station, and finding that she had gone there in a bustling way at about the time of the departure of the Sydney express, he naturally concluded that she had gone to Sydney. He then abandoned the search for her.

But she had not left the colony, as was supposed. She had merely shifted to 280 Cardigan-street, where she rented a house and furnished it upon terms at the expense of Messrs. Marks and Co. The baby-farming business was again engaged in, and without any interference from the police, until August, when Barbara Ann Davis, of Carlton, upon whom she had abandoned a child, issued a warrant for her arrest. With the issue of this warrant and the chances it promised of serious difficulties in the law courts, Thwaites cleared out for Sydney, where she was subsequently joined by her husband Knorr.

PREVIOUS HISTORY OF MRS. THWAITES.

Mrs. Thwaites is a native of Chelsea, England, and the daughter of a hat manufacturer named Thwaites, living in King's-road in that town. She came to Australia five or six years ago, and took up her residence in Sydney, where she rapidly brought herself under the notice of the police as a petty offender. After figuring several times in the police courts for trifling offences she was charged in 1888 with the larceny as a bailee of a sewing-machine. Upon that charge she was found guilty, and sentenced to 12 months' imprisonment. Soon after her release from gaol she became engaged to Rudolph Knorr, and in November, 1889, married him at St. Phillips's Church of England, Sydney.

Since that time Mrs. Knorr, or Thwaites, as she prefers to call herself, has lived with her husband in Sydney,

Adelaide, and Melbourne. Their Melbourne life dates back to about three years ago, and during much of it Mrs. Thwaites has had to maintain herself. While doing this she has maintained a correspondence with her relatives in England, and one of her letters, which was handed by her to Constable Wilcox when he was submitting her to examination, is interesting as coming from her parents-in-law to her father. It reads as follows:

"December 10, 1891.

Dear Mr. Thwaites, Last year, on the 15th May, I read a letter from my son, R. Knorr, in Melbourne, in which he told us the surprising news that he had married your dear daughter in Sydney, and that a few months later he moved to Melbourne with his dear wife. I answered his letter at once, sending him my blessing and wishes for his prosperity, but since that time we have never received any answer, so it makes us very uneasy, and we think something must have happened the young pair, and we feel very unhappy; therefore I have taken the liberty to write and ask if you know anything about them. We also thought it possible they might be living in London, and if so I am sure that if you know anything of our children you will be so kind as to let us know at once. We would be very pleased to have the honour and pleasure of making your acquaintance personally. However, that we must leave to time. We should have written to you long ago, but as I am unable to speak English it was not possible to write this note until to-day. With our kind regards, we remain, yours sincerely, CHAS. KNORR, Mrs. KNORR, and SON PAUL.

(The Argus, 7 September 1893)

ACCIDENTS IN BRUNSWICK: A WARNING TO PARENTS

The folly of parents bringing their children out with them whilst on business, and allowing them to wander from their sides during the time of heavy vehicular traffic, was in evidence on Saturday evening last, when no less than three accidents happened within half an hour of each other.

The first was to a lad named Furnessy six years of age, who resides with his parents in North Brunswick. The little fellow went to cross the road to his mother, when he was knocked down by a buggy and severely injured. He was at once removed to the Melbourne Hospital.

The second case was that of a lad named John Hall, aged 7 years, who resides with his parents in Sturrock-street, North Brunswick. The lad in endeavouring to get out of the road of a tram car was knocked down by a spring cart, driven by a young man from Coburg, who on seeing what had happened, drove straight away. On the little fellow being picked up, it was at first thought that he was killed, but close examination disclosed that he had been stunned, having received a nasty abrasion on the right temple.

The third case was a more serious one. A youth named James Shortis, of about 11 summers, a resident of Albert-street, Brunswick, was in the act of running across Ovens-street when he tripped and fell in front of a pony cart driven by a Mr. Thornton, of Ascot Vale. The wheel of the vehicle passed over the unfortunate little fellow's body, inflicting some very severe cuts to the lad's face and breaking his left arm. No blame can be attached to the driver as the lad was solely in fault.

(The Coburg Leader, 16 September 1893)

BRUNSWICK VILLAGE SETTLEMENTS

The interest taken by Mr. F. J. Sincock in trying [to] provide comfortable homes for the unemployed of Brunswick is worthy of all commendation, and deserves the hearty cooperation and support of the residents of our town.

This gentleman has opened an office at 22 Albert-street, a few doors higher up than the *Medium* Office, where any particulars concerning the scheme may be obtained. Through his agency he has secured a valuable block of land, some 2,000 acres in extent, at French Island, and has had it registered at the Lands Office. The number of local residents enrolled on the books of the Brunswick Village Settlements Homestead Association are 114, all of whom seem sanguine of the success of the undertaking, and are willing to take up a block.

A meeting was held on Wednesday evening last for the purpose of enrolling names who are willing to settle on French Island. There was a very large attendance, and 51 of the unemployed consented to go thither.

The act provides that each settler can have no more than 50 acres. They shall get the land rent free for the first three years, at a lease of 20 years, and after the expiration of the three years, the tenant will pay a yearly rental of £1 per acre half-yearly, after which time the 50 acres will become the property of the settler.

The Government will donate £15 to the settler, and a free pass to the settlement, and any person from the age of 15 years is entitled to a block. The Brunswick association have received a large number of signatures of gentlemen approving of the scheme and we feel assured that if the person who happens to take up a selection work[s] zealously the scheme must be productive of good results.

Taking a retrospective glance there is nothing to look forward to in Brunswick for some considerable time to come, whilst down at French Island there are plenty of game and fishing, so that people can live very cheaply.

(The Coburg Leader, 30 September 1893)

BICYCLE ACCIDENT AT BRUNSWICK

A man named John Morrison, residing in Albion-street, Brunswick, reported to the Brunswick police yesterday that on Saturday night, at about 8 o'clock, while crossing the Sydney-road, he was run into by a young man riding a bicycle and knocked down and very much hurt. He states that the rider was in company with several others and they were riding furiously along the Sydney-road without lights or gongs, and that before he could get out of the way he was run into and knocked down.

The riders stopped and made inquiries if any bones were broken, and then got on their machines and rode off again. Morrison finds that he is much more seriously hurt than at fast supposed, and is anxious to discover the man who caused the accident. It appears that the cyclists were some of those who had engaged in a road race to Wallan on Saturday last, and the accident occurred while they were on their way back to Melbourne.

(The Argus, 4 October 1893)

SAD DROWNING CASE

The many cases of drowning and accidents that occur in the unused clayholes in Brunswick, do not seem to be a warning to children, and it is with the sincerest regret that we have this week to publish an account of a sad drowning fatality that occurred in a clayhole belonging to Messrs Barmingham* and Lacey.

At about 5.30 p.m. on Thursday evening last, a boy named Ernest Albert Barningham, 13 years of age, and third son of Mr. Chas. Barningham, a very old and highly respected resident of Brunswick, was drowned in a clayhole between Weston and Barkly streets, East Brunswick. The little fellow, in company with another lad, went down to the water's edge, when the deceased attempted to get on a raft that was floating about in the hole, and getting one foot on it, the raft swerved from under him and he fell into the water.

An alarm was raised and Mr. Welch, butcher, hastened to the scene, and was shortly after followed by two young men named Francis Anderson and Thomas Minnifree. They all three young fellows dived in to try and find the body, and after two fruitless attempts, Anderson brought it to the surface of the water on a third attempt, but feeling exhausted, had to let it go, and the body sank again and was not recovered for some considerable time.

*Presumably should be 'Barningham'
(The Coburg Leader, 28 October 1893)

VILLAGE SETTLEMENTS: BRUNSWICK MEN ON FRENCH ISLAND

On Tuesday last Cr. King of Brunswick and Cr. Voice of Coburg, starting at a quarter to six in the morning from Brunswick arrived on the settlement at French Island at one o'clock... Mr. Glenister, the secretary, writes on 30th November: "Brockwell and Cleasby have been away getting Mutton bird eggs. Merritt took them over to Phillip Island. They brought back 40 dozen eggs and five dozen barracouta, furnishing us with plenty of provisions for a good many days. We have not enough milk – goats would be able to thrive at once – can you not get some of those removing about in the old place? Any people owning goats could give real help by leaving word at the office, have a goat in milk and this want will be more felt when our families are here. A couple of old Colonial ovens would be very valuable. We drew lots whose house was to be put up first, and it came out queer. I was the last man to draw and I got number one out of the hat. We are building the huts of wattle and dab, using the Ti-tree. The party have received a boat to be called the "Helena," after the christian name of the lady (Mrs. Minet) by whose generosity they were enabled to buy [it]..."

(The Coburg Leader, 9 December 1893)

THE ALLEGED CHILD MURDERS AT BRUNSWICK: SENSATIONAL EVIDENCE

Considerable sensation was created in the Criminal Court on Thursday last when Mrs. Thwaites, who is being tried for the child murder at Brunswick in April last, elected to go into the witness box and affirm on oath her innocence of the crime. The prisoner told a remarkable story, admitting that she had buried two children in the back yards respectively of the Moreland-road house and the Davis-street house, but said that both died from natural causes, and then she charged the man Thompson, with whom she had been on familiar terms, with strangling and burying the baby girl whose body was found at Davis-street.

Examined by counsel, the prisoner went on to say that a man named Wilson – whom the police had been unable to find – buried the child "Baby Crichton" at Moreland-road, and that she substituted another baby which had been at nurse with a "Mrs. Charlton" – also undiscoverable – and handed it over to the Crichtons as theirs. The second baby she buried herself, and it was when engaged in that work that she discovered the strangled baby, which, according to her story, disappeared one night when it had been left alone in the house with Thompson. These were the main points in a long and intricate statement, which was followed with breathless interest by a crowded court.

Thompson was re-called, and gave an emphatic denial to the prisoner's allegations concerning himself. Rudolph Knorr, prisoner's husband, who is concerned with his wife in another charge of child murder, was called but not examined.

Mr[s]. Knorr completely lost that coolness which had characterised her appearance in the dock from the opening of her trial. [S]he elected to be sworn and deny her guilt and to face cross-examination and all the accompanying risks of such a course. As she stepped from the dock to the witness box she was flushed, and her every movement indicated suppressed excitement, and as the examination went on – and particularly when she was denying any idea of doing any harm to the children – she broke into tears. She freely admitted having taken to this baby farming or baby dealing as a means of livelihood, her *modus operandi* being to take children with a premium and immediately "board them out," but of no more serious crime had she been guilty.

She asserted that the Moreland-road baby, "Baby Crichton," died from convulsions during the night, and though her first thought was to inform the police, she was too "frightened and ashamed" to go to the station, and she got Wilson to bury it. The other baby at Davis-street, she said, died from weakness, and she buried it all herself. She had to do the work quickly in order to go to the door to see a policeman who had called to tell her to register her house for taking "boarded out" children. Out of six children taken by her between April 8 and June 9 of this year, three were buried in back yards, one being buried by Thompson.

(The Coburg Leader, 2 December 1893)

THE BRUNSWICK BABY MURDERS: MRS. KNORR SENTENCED TO DEATH: MR. JUSTICE HOLROYD OFFERS NO HOPE OF REPRIEVE.

Mr. Justice Holroyd attended at the Central Criminal Court at 2 o'clock yesterday afternoon, to pass sentence upon Mrs. Frances Knorr, who was found guilty of the murder of an infant. The prisoner was brought to the court from the Melbourne Gaol in a cab, and her movements were watched with eager interest by a large crowd of onlookers. Every seat in the court was occupied, and the doors were besieged by scores of people who were unable to obtain admission. The prisoner was accompanied by a female warder, and was sobbing bitterly as she was assisted into the dock. When asked by the Judge's associate in the usual form whether she had anything to say why the Court should not pass sentence upon her according to law, the prisoner kept her face buried in her handkerchief and answered only by renewed sobbing and a shake of the head.

Mr. Justice HOLROYD speaking with great solemnity, said:- Frances Knorr, prisoner at the bar, You have been found guilty of the murder of a female child, whose name is unknown. I am not about to add to the bitterness of your position by enlarging on the enormity of your crime – one, unhappily, that could not but have been expected from the career into which you entered. The evidence against you was purely circumstantial, but such a chain of circumstances was woven around you that you could not escape from them. It is my painful duty now to pass upon you the last sentence of the law; and lest you should be encouraged to indulge in false expectations, I feel bound to say that although the prerogative of mercy does not rest with me, I cannot hold out to you any hope that your sentence will be commuted. The sentence of the Court is that you be taken from the place where you now stand to the place from whence you came, and that from that place you be taken to such gaol as His Excellency the Governor may by writing under his hand direct, and at such time as he shall direct, and that there you be hanged by the neck till you be dead, and that your body be buried in the precincts of the last gaol in which you were confined after conviction; and may the Lord have mercy on your soul.

The prisoner did not look up while his Honour was addressing her, and was assisted out of the court in a half-fainting condition. The crowd thronged the quadrangle as she was placed in the cab and driven back to the Melbourne Gaol.

(The Argus, 16 December 1893)

THE BRUNSWICK QUARTETTE: CHARGED WITH VAGRANCY: SENTENCED TO 12 MONTHS.

At the Brunswick Court on Wednesday last the Brunswick quartette consisting of Arthur Sydney Reed, Henry Hughes, Margaret Reed and Harriet Hughes stood forward to answer the charge of being idle and disorderly persons, having no lawful visible means of support.

Constable Fennessy deposed that he knew the prisoners before the Court. He had seen them coming home all hours of the night.

In answer to Harriet Hughes, he had often seen her coming home late.

Mrs. Hughes: Yes, your worship; he insulted me and tore the skirt off me.

Constable Mahony deposed that he had seen the prisoners coming home between one and two o'clock in the morning. The female prisoners had a very bad reputation. He never knew the men to work.

Constable O'Shannessy, of South Melbourne, deposed that he knew the woman Hughes who went under the name of Becher. She along with her husband, received a sentence of 12 months for keeping a house of ill-repute.

Constable Booth deposed that he arrested Reid [Reed] on the charge of assault with the intent to rob, and he was sentenced to two years imprisonment. He knew the women who were of the lowest class.

For the defence, Hughes said he had been working for three months.

Each of the prisoners were sentenced to 12 months' imprisonment.

(The Coburg Leader, 23 December 1893)

BURGLARIES AT BRUNSWICK

John Dodson, a cab proprietor, residing in Lyle-street, Brunswick, reported to the local police yesterday that during the previous night his house had been entered by thieves and the sum of £2 10s. stolen. The robbery was a most audacious one, as the burglars entered a bedroom and took the money while the informant's wife was in bed asleep.

A robbery was also committed at the premises of Henry Wallis, a draper in Carnarvon-street, amongst the articles stolen being a quantity of indiarubber hose and a cage containing three canaries, the property being valued at £3 10s.

(The Argus, 10 January 1894)

BURGLARY AT BRUNSWICK

A man named George Dickens was arrested by Constable Seddon and taken to the Brunswick Police Station at about 12 o'clock on Thursday last on a charge of attempting to steal a tap from a bathroom in a house in La Rose-street. At first the prisoner resisted and threatened the constable with a screw wrench, but on Constable Seddon presenting a revolver at him he gave himself up.

(The Coburg Leader, 13 January 1894)

THE EXECUTION OF MRS. KNORR

Frances Knorr, the Brunswick baby-farmer, who was found guilty at the last sittings of the Supreme Court of child murder, was executed in the Melbourne Gaol yesterday morning, at 10 o'clock. When the hour appointed for execution arrived about fifteen hundred people had gathered outside the gaol walls. At 10 minutes to 10 o'clock a small procession of 13 people, consisting of justices of the peace, doctors, and pressmen passed from the entrance gate to the corridor in which the gallows is situated. Several minutes later, as they stood waiting for the appearance of the sheriff, the profound silence was broken by a chorus in the condemned cell of half-a-dozen voices singing the hymn "Safe in the arms of Jesus." Two verses of that hymn were followed by several verses of "Abide with me," and when the chorus ceased, and only the voice of the chaplain, raised in prayer, could be heard, Mr. Ellis (the sheriff), Mr. Casey (the deputy sheriff), and Captain Burrowes (the governor of the gaol) appeared.

Everything was in readiness, still when the sheriff demanded the body and handed over his warrant to the governor there was a delay of a few moments longer than usual, and the spectators were apprehensive lest there should be a scene on the drop. The slight delay was accounted for by the difficulty of pinioning the woman and making certain that her skirts were all secured in such a way as to prevent the possibility of their catching in the side of the gallows. That it was not the fault, as was feared, of the woman, or of any disinclination on her part to go to her doom, was evidenced a moment later, when, preceded by the chaplain (the Rev. Mr. Scott), and guided by the hangman, Roberts, and accompanied by the medical officer of the gaol, Dr. Shields, she walked on to the drop.

Her step was firm. The few arrangements were soon complete, and the sheriff having put the usual question to the woman, "Have you anything to say?" prior to directing the drawing of the bolt, received in answer the words, "Yes; the Lord is with me. I do not fear what man can do unto me, for I have peace, perfect peace." The first sentence was spoken almost inaudibly, but the last words were delivered in a full, clear voice. The next instant the bolt was drawn, and death was instantaneous.

Amongst the documents left with Captain Burrowes by Mrs. Knorr were a confession (already noted in *The Argus*), a letter for Mr. Patterson, the Premier, on baby-farming, and suggestions for its better regulation; a letter for her mother, and a Bible with an inscription for her husband, Rudolph Knorr. The confession and the letter to the Premier were delivered to him by the sheriff immediately after the execution. The only portion of the contents which he will make available for publication is a post[s]cript added to the confession. It reads as follows:

"Jan 13, 1894.

As I feel that I have not expressed myself clearly, I now desire to state that upon the two charges known in evidence as No. 1 and 2 babies I confess to be guilty. Placed as I am now, within a few hours of my death, I express a strong desire that this statement be made public with the hope that my fate will not only be a warning to others but also act as a deterrent to those who are perhaps carrying on the same practice.

FRANCES KNORR."

(The Argus, 16 January 1894)

MYSTERIOUS DISAPPEARANCE AT BRUNSWICK

A most unaccountable disappearance of a young man named Maurice Knott, of Miller-street, Brunswick, was reported to the Brunswick police yesterday. It appears that the young man went to Melbourne and had his photograph taken last week. He also drew his money out of the bank. On Monday evening he retired to bed in his usual health, but on the following morning, at about 8 o'clock, he was suddenly missed. Upon searching his bedroom his photograph and money were found on his dressing-table. The young man has not since been seen, and his parents are alarmed at his disappearance. He is described as about 5ft. 7in. in height, of dark complexion, and clean shaved. He was dressed in a light tweed sac suit.

(The Argus, 25 January 1894)

A WELL-MERITED PUNISHMENT

At the Brunswick Court on Saturday morning, before Messrs. Crook, Fleming, and Clement, J.P.'s, two young men named Daniel Busfield and Henry Hawkins were charged with unlawfully assaulting two brothers named Frederick and Alexander Dempster. The evidence of Constables Green and Scholes showed that on the previous evening, while a party was in progress at the residence of the complainants, the defendants, who were in an intoxicated condition, entered the place without an invitation, and conducted themselves in a most disgraceful manner, assaulting the brothers Dempster as well as some of their guests, including a lady. Their proceedings were so outrageous that the police were sent for, and the two men arrested. Sergeant Brown informed the Bench that it was not the first time the prisoners had been before the Court for a similar offence. Both men pleaded guilty, and advanced intoxication as an excuse for their conduct. They were each fined £10, or in default three months' imprisonment.

(The Argus, 12 February 1894)

AN UNLUCKY FAMILY

A rather serious accident, and one which, it is feared, will have a fatal termination, occurred at Brunswick on Tuesday afternoon last, whereby a man named James Leury sustained very serious injuries.

It appears that Leury for some purpose at present unexplained, climbed to the top of an unused brick kiln adjoining his house in Victoria-street, owned by Mr. Roche, and by some means fell to the ground. His groans were heard by some passers by, and upon going to [the] spot they found the man lying unconscious and much injured.

They conveyed him home and Dr. Overend was sent for, and upon his examining Leury, he found that he had received an injury to the spine as well as the head, and his face was much cut about, and he is now under medical treatment.

The Leury family have been most unfortunate during the past year or two. About two and a half years ago their house was burnt down through the adjoining house catching fire. About twelve months ago two of their children were drowned in an abandoned quarryhole, and about five months ago Leury was seriously hurt by being thrown from a horse which he was riding.

(The Coburg Leader, 17 March 1894)

SUICIDE AT WEST BRUNSWICK

On the evening of Easter Monday, a resident of West Brunswick named McColville went to Senior Constable Stoddart and informed him that Mr. Charles Henry Parker, a well-known engine driver, had committed suicide by hanging himself with a clothes line in a washhouse at his residence in Barry-street, West Brunswick. The senior constable hastened to the place and found that the story was too true for he found the body of the unfortunate man suspended to a rafter in the washhouse. From the appearance of the body the senior constable thought that death must have occurred four or five hours before.

The district coroner was communicated with and an inquest was held on Wednesday, the 28th inst., at Nolan's Hotel, Union-street. Janet Parker was the first witness examined, and said that the deceased was her father. She last saw him alive on the forenoon of Easter Monday, a little before 12 o'clock. Her sister and her self were going out to spend the day and at the back door he said "good bye" to them. There was nothing unusual in his manner. He had been low spirited and depressed. He had been out of work for about 18 months and had tried to get work but failed. He sometimes could not sleep, and walked up and down the house talking to himself.

Their youngest brother had left the house before they did, and their father was the only one left in the house. He often threatened to take his own life but they never thought he would do it. There were five children in the family. On the previous day (Sunday) he said "Your mother died on New Year's Day and I will die on Easter Monday." The writing on the slate (produced) "Look in the washhouse," was in her father's handwriting. There was no other writing or any thing left. On her return about a quarter before 8 p.m. her father was dead.

Angus Henry Parker, a son of the deceased, aged 11 years, said that he left home, above on the morning of Easter Monday. He was going to Brighton Beach with Mr. Harrison. His father was at home. He looked bad. He said "Good bye." Witness returned about half past four or five o'clock and did not find any one in the house. He went into the back kitchen and saw his father's hat lying on the table and a slate on the top of it. There was written on the slate in his father's handwriting, "Look in the washhouse." He went to the washhouse and he saw his father hanging. He ran to a neighbour, Mr. McColville, and told him and he (Mr. McColville) went to Senr.-Constable Stoddart. He said to Mr. McColville, "My father is stiff, hanging there." His father did not drink at all. He never heard his father say he would take his own life. He was low spirited. There was no disturbing words with his father on the morning they went away.

Wm. Stoddart, Senr.-Constable of police, stationed at

Brunswick, said Mr. MoColville came to him on the evening of the 26th, and told him that Mr. Parker had hanged himself. Witness hastened to the place and found deceased hanging to a rafter of the washhouse. The body was cold and stiff and seemed to have been dead about four or five hours. There were no signs of any straggle and the body was partly clothed with trousers, vest and boots. They did not seem to be disturbed since the putting of them on.

After the coroner had summed up the evidence the jury found that "deceased committed suicide while in an unsound state of mind."

(The Coburg Leader, 31 March 1894)

SERIOUS ACCIDENT AT BRUNSWICK

A peculiar but very serious accident happened at Brunswick on Saturday morning, resulting in a youth named Edgar Bons, aged 16, son of the licensee of the Cumberland Arms Hotel, receiving a very dangerous wound on his head. It appears that the youth, with some of his brothers, was pitching a portion of the yard. One of them was using a heavy pick for the purpose, one similar to those used by railway navvies with a blunt head. The boys were working close together, and as the pick was raised the boy Edgar stooped to get one of the stones, with the result that the pick descended and struck him a heavy blow on the head, which felled him to the ground.

He was found to be seriously hurt, and upon Dr. Miller examining him he found that he had sustained a very serious fracture of the skull, and it is very doubtful if he will recover from his injuries. At a late hour last night the operation of trephining was performed by Dr. Miller.

(The Argus, 2 April 1894)

ALLEGED COINING AT BRUNSWICK: A MAN ARRESTED

An important arrest was made by Sergeant Percival and Constables Simmonds and Wilcox, of the Brunswick police, on Saturday morning, when a man named John Anderson, aged 30 years, was apprehended upon a charge of coining. For the past two or three days complaints have been made by business people on the Sydney-road that they had been victimised by a person passing base shillings upon them.

The inquiries of the police cast suspicion on Anderson, who has been kept under surveillance for some time. On Saturday morning, from further information received, the police decided to arrest him. When searched at the lock-up he had no money of any description upon him, but a search of the premises occupied by him disclosed in one of the rooms a regular coiner's outfit, consisting of a light portable furnace, dies for making and impressing shillings, as well as a quantity of a white metal which had been reduced in the furnace. The stuff was apparently made from watch-cases, as a number of these were found on the premises. A quantity of chemicals was also discovered. No money of any kind was found during the search.

(The Argus, 9 April 1894)

A CHILD KIDNAPPED BY ITS MOTHER: ARREST OF THE WOMAN IN THE CHINESE QUARTER

A strange report of kidnapping was recently brought under the notice of the police at Carlton, and yesterday led to the arrest of a woman named Annie Thomas on the peculiar charge of stealing her own child.

It appears that somewhere about three years ago the police had the woman Thomas under their observation. She was gaining a livelihood in an uncertain and precarious way, and as she had a little girl child named after herself, Annie Thomas, the police concluded that the interests of the child would be best served by having her looked after in the neglected children's department.

Accordingly the little girl was arrested and brought before the police court as a neglected child. Mr Thomas Byrne, of 1 Louisa-street, Brunswick, was present in the court at the time and offered to adopt her under the provisions of the Infant Life Protection Act 1890. The Bench made inquiries as is usual, respecting Mr Byrne's position and character, and, being abundantly satisfied, passed the child over to him as desired. Nothing more was heard of the matter outside the routine of the neglected children's department until recently, when a strange woman was observed loitering about Mr Byrne's house. Her conduct was not then heeded much, as neither Mr Byrne nor his firmly had the faintest suspicion that she had any connection with the little girl now become part of the household.

On Wednesday, the 20th inst., however, the child disappeared. She had been playing round about the house, and was seen a few minutes before her disappearance. Inquiries in the neighbourhood showed that the strange woman had been again observed that day watching Mr Byrne's house. After a painstaking investigation someone was found who had seen the woman first talk to the child and then walk away with her down the street. The police were communicated with, and ultimately a warrant was issued for the arrest of the woman Annie Thomas on the charge of "having unlawfully induced Annie Thomas, a ward of the neglected children's department, to abscond from the home of Mr. Thomas Byrne, of Brunswick."

The police had no difficulty in tracing the accused woman. They found her living in a house in Rathdown[e]-street, Carlton, but the child could not be seen, and the most careful questioning of the neighbours and patient watching of the woman's movements would not reveal to the detectives her hiding place.

After several days vainly spent in this way the arrest of the woman was decided upon. Accordingly Detective Britt went yesterday to a house frequented by Chinese in Little Lonsdale-street, and there found the woman with others of low character. There was no sign of the child there, and Britt took the woman with him in a search of other Chinese dens. In one of these there was trouble. His intrusion was resented, and he was set upon by several of the occupants of the house. His prisoner, who had not been handcuffed, joined in the struggle, and Britt was rapidly getting the worst of the fight when Constable Trainor went to his assistance and rescued him. The detective carried away painful evidences of his encounter in the shape of a bleeding hand, a dislocated thumb, and torn and disarranged clothing. The accused will appear at the City Court today.

(The Argus, 25 June 1894)

SUSPICIOUS DEATH AT BRUNSWICK

Dr. Robertson, of Rathdowne-street, Carlton, reported to Sergeant Brown at Brunswick yesterday afternoon that a young woman named Elizabeth Alford, residing at 62 Cassell-road, Moreland, had died at about 5 o'clock that morning under somewhat suspicious circumstances. He stated that he was called in to attend the deceased last Sunday evening, when he found her in a moribund condition, and he visited her daily, but she gradually sank, and died as stated.

Deceased was 28 years of age, and unmarried. She was a native of Mortlake, and had been a domestic servant, until recently in the employment of a Mrs. Stevens, of Moreland-road. Mrs. Stevens stated that a few days ago deceased complained of being very ill, and admitted having taken some drugs. She (Mrs. Stevens) advised her to go and get medical advice, and upon her recommendation went to a nurse named Mrs. Peachey, at whose house she was residing when she died.

Mrs. Peachey has informed the police that when she charged the deceased with having taken drugs she admitted it, and said she had obtained them at Carlton, but she refused to state who from, and she also said that she had paid as much as £5 for some of the medicine she had taken. The police are at present investigating the matter...

(The Argus, 19 July 1894)

BURGLARS FOILED

A sensational attempted burglary was reported to the Brunswick police on Tuesday last by Mr. Otto Nenendorf, photographer, who resides with his wife and family at Cassell's-road, Brunswick.

Mr. Nenendorf states that he awoke at about three o'clock on the morning in question, and noticed through his bedroom door, which was partly open, the reflection of a light in the passage. He rushed into the passage where he saw three men, one of whom carried a candle. The latter was immediately extinguished and the men ran out into the back yard through the kitchen door, which they had opened.

Mr. Nenendorf pursued them, one of whom ran into an outhouse, and the other bailed up in one corner in the yard, upon Mr. Nenendorf requesting him to do so.

By the aid of moonlight, however they were made aware that their pursuer was unarmed, and the two men rushed from the outhouse and climbed over the fence. The man who had stood in the corner of the yard did likewise, but before scaling the fence, drew a revolver and deliberately pointing at Mr. Nenendorf, fired. The shot fortunately was not a true one, although the intended victim heard the bullet whiz by close to him.

It was afterwards discovered that entrance to the house had been gained by forcing open a window in which a child slept, over whose face the burglars had placed a cloth with the idea probably of hiding the light.

It was evident the thieves had just entered the house, as nothing was disturbed.

(The Coburg Leader, 18 August 1894)

THE BOOTMAKERS STRIKE

At about five o'clock yesterday evening, some 500 bootmakers, who are on strike for higher wages, assembled at the factory of Mr. S. King, Albert-street, Brunswick, with the intention of "doing for" what they term blacklegs. The

Unionists waited until the men had knocked off, and by this time fully 2000 persons must have assembled and the utmost excitement prevailed.

On knocking off time arriving, the boys employed by Mr. King wended their way towards the Sydney-road, whilst the men proceeded Lygon-street way. The Unionists followed them hooting and jeering them, until they reached home. The men then assembled on a vacant allotment of land, and letters were read out purporting to be signed by Mr. King, asking his men to return to work, which Mr. King denied, and offered a reward to any person who could prove he asked the men to return to work.

At this stage great excitement was created, and the men hooting and jeering wended their way towards Carlton, followed by about a dozen police.

(The Coburg Leader, 18 August 1894)

RUSHED BY A COW

An accident of rather a peculiar nature, and which subsequently had a fatal termination, happened at Brunswick on Friday evening. A little girl named Annie Hicks, about 9 years of age, was returning home from school in company with several other children, and when near Princes-park on the Sydney-road a cow, which was being driven from Melbourne by a boy named Ford, rushed at her, throwing her heavily on the road and rendering her insensible. She was taken to her home in Park-street, and her injuries were of such a character that she died at about 4 o'clock on Saturday afternoon. The cow was a very wild one, and shortly after rushing the deceased attacked the lad Ford, who was driving it, knocking him down and breaking his arm.

(The Argus, 24 September 1894)

PETITIONING THE BRUNSWICK COUNCIL: A MISERABLE FREAK

At the Brunswick council meeting held on Monday evening last, a petition signed by some 160 ratepayers was read, asking the council in some way or another to provide them with work by giving them turn about with the men employed by the council at the present time, laying great stress on the scavenging work.

Cr. Cook thought that men competent enough to do the work could be obtained in Brunswick, and was of opinion that they should have turn about with the men at present employed by the council. He would move that the letter would be referred to the minimum rate of wage committee.

Cr. Allard seconded the motion. He thought a lot of "bunkum" had been spoken over this subject that night. They did not want men with a University education to survey the channels.

Cr. Methven could not see why they should refer it to the committee. It can be settled in a minute. It meant spending money. If they were to appoint a new man and an old one they would find that the old man would be at the bottom of the street at the night and the new one at the top. If the council approve of this they will place themselves in a very awkward position as regards who are to be put on the work first. You would find men hanging round after you asking why they were not put on. It was an utter absurdity.

Cr. Fleming hoped that those councillors who were anxious to get the men on would find money to pay them. The council cannot pay its men now.

Cr. Allard - Is that a fact Mr. Mayor?

Cr. Fleming - It is a fact, Cr. Allard, and you can't deny it. There is not a penny on the notice paper to-night for them. The way the council was going on it would take them all there [their] time to pay costs. If the council dismiss 14 men and put 14 out of that list on, someone would come and say, "Why did you not put me on."

Cr. Talbot said the council attached too much importance to this note. He read a motion which he argued that men owing money to the council should be employed and a percentage deducted from their wages to pay their indebtedness when that motion was put it was lost, and now some councillors who voted against it have turned completely round and gone on the other side. They have a weakness and their knees bend to any side. The system has been tried as far back as 500 years ago by men with better heads than any sitting at this table and has proved a failure. The ratepayers will regret the day they ever brought forward such a scheme and he was sorry that he was taking part in the discussion. It was made a parrot cry by parliamentary candidates to gain a point, and a miserable point it was. He had voted against the minimum rate of wage principal and would do so again and if the ratepayers were not satisfied, they could throw him out, he was not particular; but he hoped they would get someone to vote as conscientiously as he did.

Cr. Hearn had heard it said from men who signed the petition that they would not see one man put off for him to be put on.

Cr. Hennessy said a lot of heat had been infused into the discussion. It was a wide matter and a hard thing to deal with. There were a lot of old men in the district, and if they were employed they would manage to pay their rates.

Cr. Cook thought the letter wanted serious consideration and hoped that it would be referred to the committee.

Cr. Methven moved, as an amendment, that the surveyor be empowered to employ 1, 2, 3 or 4 men every 14 days.

Cr. Cook said that the resolution was of no use. No machinery in it. He thought it was moved in a fit of plaguy.

Cr. Fleming rose to a point of order and demanded a withdrawal of the sentiment.

Cr. Cook said he thought such was the case, but would withdraw the remarks and apologise.

The amendment was lost.

Cr. Talbot moved that the engineer be instructed to dismiss seven of the council's employees and put on seven other ratepayers, and so on every fortnight, until all the unemployed in the town willing to work received work.

Cr. Fleming seconded the motion, which was carried.

Cr. Talbot demanded a division with the following result: For the motion, Crs. Talbot, Miller, Hearn, Fleming and Methven; against Crs. Cook, Allard, Hennessy.

Cr. Talbot - Why you are voting against the very thing you are requiring.

Cr. Cook - I am nothing of the sort. I know what I want.

The matter then dropped.

(The Coburg Leader, 13 October 1894)

THE CHINESE DEVIL-DODGER AND THE BRUNSWICK BELL

What will society think when a leading almond-eye resident by his conduct, demonstrates that Cupid's arrow has penetrated his bosom. This intellectual visitant from the Celestial land has during the past ten days followed and intercepted a beautiful Christian young lady, whom necessity compels to visit Melbourne on business. There is no mistaking the design of the Chinaman, as he proposed honourable marriage to the maiden. Can we then blame him when his intentions are honourable? "Love laughs at bolts and bars when they are material," why not when they are bars of Race?

Suffice it is to say that the young lady has told her mother, and the foreign friend received his *conge* one evening during the week within close proximity to Blyth-street. The gay Lothario has lost in weight since and gained a dejected expression of countenance, so it must be until China has conquered first Japan and then England.

(The Coburg Leader, 27 October 1894)

THE FATALITY AT BRUNSWICK

The sad accident at West Brunswick in the Phoenix-park clay-hole of the Hoffman Brick Company, which caused the death on Tuesday of William and James Storen, two pipeclay workers in the employ of the company, formed the subject of an investigation yesterday by the coroner for Bourke, Mr. Candler.

Mr Hickford appeared on behalf of the widows of the two men.

Stephen England, manager of the Hoffman Steam Tile and Brick Company, stated that the two deceased had worked for the company for about 15 years. They were sober and industrious, and their experience in working pipeclay was considerable. The accident appeared to be due to the undermining of the bank, and knowing the risks of such working he had repeatedly cautioned the men against it. In this case the accident was due to the act of the men themselves, and no one else was to blame.

After other evidence the jury returned a verdict that the deceased were accidentally killed by a fall of pipeclay, and added that there was not sufficient evidence to show how the fall occurred.

(The Argus, 15 November 1894)

ROLLED IN RAGS

Two females named Mary Dickens and Elizabeth Ah Kin, *alias* Eliza Fitzpatrick were each charged at the Brunswick court on Wednesday morning last with having no lawful visible means of support.

Constable Wilcox deposed that on the night of the 25th inst, from information received, he went to a chinaman's garden in Albion-street, Brunswick. He stood some distance away, and saw the two defendants knock at the Chinaman's house and enter. He went nearer the hut and heard female voices. He knocked at the door and two Chinamen came out. He asked where the women were, and he replied "no woman here." He then went inside and on a bedroom door being opened, another Chinaman appeared. Witness asked where the women were, and met the same reply. He entered the bedroom and found Dickens hidden away rolled up in a lot of rags under a bed. He knew her to be a common prostitute and a constant inhabitant of Chinese dens in the town. The two women knocked about the road all hours of the night in bad company.

The woman Fitzpatrick stated she resided with Ah Kin as his wife. She took in washing and earned about 10s. per week.

The bench sentenced Dickens to six months imprisomeot [imprisonment] and discharged the other accused with a caution.

(The Coburg Leader, 30 March 1895)

OUR SOLDIERS AT BRUNSWICK

The manoeuvres of the troops on Easter Monday, were witnessed by a great number of residents of Brunswick who took occasion of the nearness of the battle ground, to form picnic parties on the sloping fields of Moreland and Brunswick West and thus obtain a splendid view of the operations carried on in this portion of the valley of Moonee Ponds Creek; spectators from the city and other suburbs were there and the gathering on the hill where the final assault was made.

The day was delightful, but the display could not arouse any military feeling, conversation among the crowds being mostly of the sewer disaster, the picnics, final cricket matches, and the opening of the football season. When the "cease fire" was sounded, much attention was paid to the officers who came from all directions to give a full account at the head quarters tent to the commander, so that there should be no mistake which side had won.

However, it was decided by court martial that the commander of the enemy, Colonel Robertson, had not injured the approaches to Brunswick in the north west, and therefore, the supplies would still be within the reach of all.

The troops after marching and manoeuvring for a distance of 18 miles marched down the Sydney-road, singing and stepping out briskly to the bands that accompanied them.

(The Coburg Leader, 20 April 1895)

THE ESCAPED LEPER: CAPTURED AT BRUNSWICK

The leper, Ah Song, who escaped from the lazaretto at Point Nepean on Tuesday night, and whose journey towards Melbourne threw the whole of the Chinese community into consternation, and the detectives, police, and Health department into a fever of unrest, was unexpectedly captured at Brunswick yesterday.

Constable Lawford, of Russell-street, was in Brunswick searching for Ah Jow, who escaped from the City Court a few days ago. Every Chinaman who was seen was hailed, and at last one did not wait to be hailed. As soon as he saw the constable he ran. Lawford pursued him and caught him, and to his astonishment found that he was the leper, Ah Song.

Lawford has seldom had a more awkward prisoner. He drove him first to the Melbourne Hospital, where the attendants looked at him in horror, and said, "Take him away – anywhere you like, but not here." The watchhouses would not receive him, and at last the constable drove to the Health department. Dr. Gresswell was not in, and Lawford took the leper to the Bourke-street west watchhouse, and keeping him in the cab quietly awaited instructions.

Dr. Gresswell subsequently ordered that the man should be locked in one of the cells and returned to Point Nepean next morning. So that he shall not again escape, three men in eight-hour shifts will be employed to watch him. Though not much danger is apprehended from the Chinaman's wanderings, Dr Gresswell has issued instructions for certain measures to be taken which should remove all chance of infection.

(The Argus, 10 May 1895)

THE BRUNSWICK MATRIMONIAL PUZZLE

A somewhat extraordinary development of the case of the deceased man Vlasoplas, to whom on Saturday two wives laid claim, took place yesterday. The Brunswick police, acting under instructions from the curator of intestate estates, went to the Greek's late residence on Sydney-road to make an inventory of his estate, and in the course of this Mrs. Vlasoplas volunteered the statement that if she was not the lawful widow of the deceased man, although she had gone through the marriage ceremony with him, then neither was the lady who had claimed that position on Saturday, and who had said that she had been married to Vlasoplas in Greece. As a matter of fact Vlasoplas was married to a woman in Liverpool before he met either of the present wives, and he married the Greek lady while the Liverpool wife was yet living. The only effect of this statement is to make the position of the two women somewhat more invidious than it was before.

(The Argus, 16 May 1895)

THE PROCESSION

The procession was fully one mile and a half in length, and was composed of grotesque sights and mirth provoking displays.

Between the hours of 8 and 10 o'clock the vicinity of the Quarry hotel was the scene of great confusion. Horsemen riding all over the place, vehicles running about here and there, and the committee running about in costume arranging matters, made everything appear as if we were in other lands than poverty stricken Brunswick.

Punctually at 10 o'clock Marshall J. Millward, dressed in his costume of King George IV, and mounted on his prancing bay steed, supported by Marshall P. Tierney and Cr. D. Methven had all in order. The East Brunswick Band held pride of place in the East, and in recognition of the honor they played their best and looked their smartest. Then came the quarrymen's banner fixed to Mr. Orchard's lorry. The procession wended its way down Barkly-street to Miller-street, up Edward-street to Lygon-street, thence to Albion-street and along the Sydney road to Moreland, where a large concourse of people had gathered to witness the proceedings.

The following took part in the procession:

The Chicken Raisers Band was indeed very funny. They carried a banner on which was painted two negro chicken stealers entering a fowl house. This was arranged by G. Sturrock and party.

The Convict Gang was got up by W. Anderson and secured second prize. It took the form of six convicts wearing costumes, chained together and "diamond cracking," drawn on a four-in-hand lorry kindly lent by the Victoria Brewery,

G. Sturrock had some twenty men rigged up in wooden helmets and hatchets.

Kitchen's candle factory, with three waggons dressed in candles and some 20 men in costume, each carrying a candle, looked very well.

Messrs White and Wallace's Darktown* blacksmith's shop (re-constructed) was well got up.

The following horsemen in costume took part:

C Sturrock, Charles Surface. W Truscott, Kings Jester. E Millward, Don Caesar De Bazan. D. Dick Jnr., Sir Walter Raleigh. G Methven, H Mindner and J Shields, Indians. J Cowley had a bullock in a cart representing a country butcher. P Tierney, Naval Officer. W Admans, the fat man from Geelong. F Admans, Ballet girl. W Belott, Captain Fritz. W. Appleby, rabbit hawker. Mr Morris, game keeper. Messrs F Bowers as Mary Ann and J Bartlet as Mr O'Rafferty at the fair with a baby in a "pram." These two gentleman gained great favor, and were awarded the second prize for the most original character. J Reith, jockey. J Dawson, huntsman. A Muirhead, Spanish Cavalier. A Sturrock, Cavalier.

Three Star Tobacco was well got up and was represented by Messrs Martin Bros and Cook.

Messrs Ford Bros Darktown laundry created endless amusement, and was well made up.

The Scorchers were mounted on a lorry and looked

fit to pull a house down. A Ford as a darkey clown and D Dolphin as the Gaiety Girl were well got up.

Ford Bros beautiful decorated cart, the first prize winner, was a feature of the procession.

T Naismith, Arab Pasha. W Jones, Stanley the explorer. H Ellis, Kings Jester. C Bourne, Spanish bull fighter. J Harding, game gatherer. A McConochie, court jester. A Pleasance, Robinson Cruso; his man Friday, J Fraser. The South African Negroes with Missionary, H Volkmer.

The Children of the East were tastefully arranged by Mr Millward.

B Willis, milkman. J Nichols, jockey. A Brown, Irishman. A darktown band of some thirty performers…

J Bradford had a miniature mia-mia erected on a waggon, and which came in for a large share of praise, winning the first prize.

E Hemingway was awarded the first prize for the best sustained character, and richly deserved it. His show was "off to Coolgardie." J Finnigan took the part of his wife and Messrs Munro and Thomas his children. He had with him his favourite parrot and his old dog Fido.

H A Friedborg as the organ grinder was well got up and secured third prize.

Mr. Bones had two lorries dressed representing "Women up to date." The whole performance of bottling draft ale was shown, while Miss Bones livened the proceedings with selections on the piano.

The Darktown fire brigade was as funny as ever…

Forty bicyclists were arrayed in different costumes and looked very well.

Darktown shoeing forge, W. Robinson, erected on a lorry making horse shoes on the road.

Mr Myers secured second prize for his dressed vehicle.

A beautiful representation of Charity was in the line.

W Wright, burnt out. J Goding, Robin Hood. Native of Jerusalem with his son and servant, Mr Waugh and Sons. H Watters representing hard times – Swell, E Watters; wife, A Rise; and daughter, T Isell.

The Darktown concept appears to be a racist lampooning of black (presumably African-American) culture, probably including blackface.
(The Coburg Leader, 1 June 1895)

STREET ROWDYISM AT BRUNSWICK
At the Brunswick Police Court on Wednesday, a young man named Elijah Stranger was charged with using obscene language on Sydney-road on the 9th inst. The evidence of Sergeant Percival showed that Stranger had had an altercation with another man, during which he had used language of a disgusting nature. Stranger attempted to justify himself by stating that the man in question had insulted him, but the Bench held that this only aggravated the offence, and inflicted a fine of £5, in default one month.

At the same court Alexander Marquiss was charged with assaulting another young man named Albert Pledger. The latter, it appeared, was standing on Sydney-road talking with some friends, when defendant with two others came up and threw a potato at Pledger. When asked why he did that Marquiss struck Pledger several blows on the face and offered to fight him. The chairman, Mr. S. King, remarked that these young fellows appeared to think that the road was their own, and that they were privileged to challenge everybody on it. A fine of 10s. with 2s. 6d. costs was imposed, in default three days' imprisonment.
(The Argus, 3 June 1895)

POLICE NEWS
Mrs. Elizabeth Seymour of Hanover street West Brunswick proceeded against Mrs. Susie Drake her next door neighbour, on a charge of administering poison to her poultry, on the first inst. by which she has lost 81 fowls. The complainant had reported the matter to Constable Dyson, who had taken one of the birds to Mr. Blackett the

Government Analyst, who on examination found that the fowl had been poisoned by arsenic. Mr. Hickford appeared for the informant, Mr. Shannon for the defendant. By consent this case was adjourned for one week as Mr. Blackett was engaged at another court on that day and could not attend to give professional evidence.

The same parties, Seymour and Drake, had two other cases, and cross summonses in which defendant charged Mrs. Seymour with threatening her life, and also wilful damage to property. The same legal talent was engaged in all cases. A third case was the first heard where Mrs Seymour charged Mrs. Drake with inciting the dog to destroy some of her poultry. The plaintiff stated that on 23 of November, Richard Drake threw a large red dog over her fence, into her yard, the dog killed 8 ducks and ran away with two of them in its mouth. Mr. Shannon cross examined the witness who said it was about 7.30 when Drake threw the dog over, witness then said to him that she would make him sit up. The dog ate four ducks and took two of them away. The defendant denied the charge, the case was dismissed.

(The Coburg Leader, 7 December 1895)

CHILD ABANDONMENT

At about 10 minutes to 12 on Saturday night James P. Lonnegan, of Park-street Brunswick, informed Senior-constable Nolan that he had discovered a female child lying on the door-mat at the residence of his neighbour, Mr. Milligan, who is at present away from home. Nolan, in company with Constables Green and Seddon, proceeded to the spot. The infant was clad in a long white calico robe, white flannel, calico and flannel napkins, and was wrapped in a large towel. A feeding bottle, containing milk, was also lying by its side. The outcast, which appears to be about one week old, was removed to the police station, and inquiries are being made as to the whereabouts of the parents.

(The Argus, 13 January 1896)

THE ATTEMPTED SUICIDE AT BRUNSWICK

Mrs. McGee, the woman who on Monday attempted to commit suicide at her residence, Whitby-street, Brunswick, by swallowing chlorodyne, was charged with the offence at the Brunswick Police Court yesterday. The case was heard privately by Messrs. Fleming and Methven, J. P.'s. It appeared that the woman had been sent to the hospital, and since her discharge therefrom had been wandering about the town, and a remand of seven days for medical examination was applied for. A sister of Mrs. McGee, named Farrell, offered to take charge of the unfortunate woman, who was accordingly committed to her care.

(The Argus, 13 March 1896)

THE BRUNSWICK SHOOTING CASE: A PECULIAR DEVELOPMENT

The police at Brunswick were of opinion that they had yesterday reached an important stage in the investigation of the circumstances of the case of shooting which occurred at the Caledonian Hotel, East Brunswick, on Tuesday week last. They arrested a man on suspicion, and for the purpose of settling the question of identity took him before Mr. McConachie, who was shot. Mr. McConachie had no hesitation in declaring that the suspect had nothing to do with the case. The man was at once discharged from the formal custody.

It was ascertained last week that a man answering the description of the "bush larrikin" who is wanted for the crime of shooting at Mr. McConachie purchased a revolver and cartridges at Michael's pawn office in Elizabeth-street on the day of the shooting. He described himself as from the country, and intimated that he was returning to the country again and wanted the revolver to shoot rabbits. The man has probably got away into the bush, and it is extremely improbable that he will ever be found.

(The Argus, 17 June 1896)

AN ORANGE RIOT: STREET FIGHTING AT BRUNSWICK: THE BATTLE OF THE RIVAL FACTIONS: HEADS BROKEN AT CHURCH DOORS

It is just 50 years since the last Orange riot took place in Melbourne, and the peaceful portion of the community had begun to feel entitled to hope that the disgraceful faction fighting of 1846 would never be renewed in Victoria. Yesterday, however, a fresh outburst of violence in Brunswick, on a scale of far greater magnitude, and embracing a much larger number of participants, showed that the flame of the old rancour, so far from having become extinct, still burns with undiminished fury.

For about three hours yesterday the extraordinary spectacle was witnessed of Protestants and Catholics – the majority of whom were natives of Australia – fighting with the ferocity of wild beasts for a politico-religious principle which has no *raison d'etre* outside of Ireland. During the height of the disturbance there could not have been fewer than 25,000 persons present, and the savage determination with which the fighting was carried on, in defiance of the efforts of about 50 constables, showed that the seed of the old *odium theologicum* has flourished with surprising vigour even in a country of specially secularised institutions. The trouble arose out of the declared intention of the local Orange Lodge to hold a service in the Wesleyan Church in commemoration of the anniversary of the Battle of the Boyne, it having been arranged that the members of the lodge should march thither in regalia.

When the chief commissioner of police early last week drew the attention of Councillor Methven, the mayor of Brunswick, to the fact that the proposed procession was illegal according to section 10 of the Unlawful Assemblies Act, it was considered probable in Brunswick that the procession of Orangemen which had been arranged for would not take place. At the same time an unobtrusive advertisement appeared in the daily newspapers inciting the Irishmen of Melbourne and suburbs to meet at 2 o'clock on the vacant piece of ground near the Sarah Sands Hotel, Brunswick.

Mr M O'Shea, who signed the advertisement, is evidently a methodical person, and he was careful to explain the object of the meeting, for the advertisement concluded with the following significant observation: - "Business – To discuss the Irish question." In consequence of this thoughtful little action on the part of Mr. O'Shea, supplemented by the partiality of many persons who happened to find themselves in the neighbourhood of Brunswick yesterday for yellow ties, handkerchiefs, ribbons, and floral decorations, the Irish question was discussed with much heat and vigour, and many blackthorns and shillelaghs.

At half past 1 o'clock the vacant piece of ground near the Sarah Sands Hotel was vacant indeed. Occasionally a casual bicyclist flew past or a belated cab rumbled back to the city, but otherwise the charming little city of Brunswick metaphorically slumbered, wrapped in its own virtue. Presently the tramp of heavy feet resounded on the pavement, and 18 foot constables, escorted by one mounted trooper, took up a strategical position on a handy corner, where a few small boys gathered to see and to admire.

The next arrival was a Yarra bank orator, who brought his red flag with him and pitched it on a vacant spot where it was evidently the custom to dump all kinds of rubbish. He urged all Protestants and Catholics present to sink their religious differences and unite against their common foe, the capitalist, but the Protestants and Catholics who had begun to assemble simply turned their backs on him, and shook their sticks in anticipatory ecstasy. An elderly cabman made use of a shocking expression in a very loud tone of voice to the orator, and then drove away blaspheming, but the orator continued perseveringly, and for two solid hours, while the tide of fight rolled past him, he continued to lift up his voice against the capitalist, the monopolist, the existing social system, and the private ownership of land. One could not but wonder at the man's enthusiasm, and his capacity for abstracting himself from the actual and present to the unreal and impossible.

Yet there was a curious touch of bizarre appositeness about some of his remarks, which could be heard above the shouts of the fighting fanatics in front of him. When an old lady had been thrown down by the mob, and was in imminent danger of being crushed to pieces until three or four stalwart fellows formed a ring round her, and kept the people back with their fists, the discordant monotone of the Yarra bank orator was heard above the din. "If this is what civilisation teaches us," yelled the neglected apostle of anarchy with considerable force, "then the sooner the present civilisation is swept away the better." But his words fell on deaf ears, and the only comment upon his observations fell from the lips of a young man who explained to a companion in the simple dialect of Collingwood that "the bloke was ratty."

HOW THE RIOT COMMENCED.

Soon after 2 o'clock the open space in front of the Sarah Sands Hotel was crowded with persons of all ages and sexes, who spread from the footpath on the one side across the tram track to the hoardings on the other. Boys perched on the tops of the hoardings like sparrows on a wall, and filled every available niche whence a view could be obtained from roof and tree and lamp post. In the street the mass meeting of Irishmen was constituted informally, and had it not been for the fact that every second man present had a piece of green ribbon in his coat and a blackthorn in his hand no one would have suspected that a political gathering was preparing "to discuss the Irish question." The crowd extended for about half a mile down the main street, where buggies, cabs, and bicycles moved slowly and cautiously through the press of the people, who had come out in their thousands to enjoy a "pleasant Sunday afternoon" of the very latest description.

Presently a drag drawn by four chestnuts and filled with Orangemen and Orangewomen, sporting the colours of their order, drove briskly up from town, and there was a low threatening growl from the pedestrians. But the psychological moment passed, and so did the drag, without a more forcible protest, though it was stopped further down by the church, where rude hands were laid on the hated emblems, and those who wore them.

However, the people were beginning to get restless, like animals when they smell blood, and the approach of the next vehicle was eagerly awaited. It came at last – an open buggy containing four men, who all showed orange rosettes. No one could say with absolute certainty exactly what happened, but from the front of an adjacent cab one could see a sudden attack by a party of men armed with stout sticks, a momentary repulse, a renewed assault, a rearing horse, and a capsizing buggy. The sticks were going with extraordinary rapidity as the four men standing up in the buggy dealt out their blows, while the weapons of their assailants came upon their heads and shoulders with a straight up and down chopping motion, delivered with a kind of half-arm blow, which was necessitated by the crush.

One in a belltopper was especially conspicuous in the attack, but the Orangemen held the position, although blood was flowing freely from their heads, until the plunging horse, maddened by the ill-aimed blows, which missed their aim and rained down upon his haunches, fell in the middle of the road. Here and there in the crowd the black helmets of the constables could be seem bobbing up and down like corks in the sea, as they attempted to shoulder their way to the scene of the disturbance; but none of them got near the buggy, and in a few moments a volley of stone metal, supplemented by another attack with the blackthorns, did severe damage to the Orangemen.

To overturn the buggy was an easy task for the mob, and the occupants, bruised and bleeding, had their detested colours torn from them by 20 pairs of eager hands. Wm. McDonald and a man named O'Sullivan were very severely injured, the former by a blow from a piece of bluestone, and the latter by a stick.

EXCITING INCIDENTS.

After this episode the mob became quite unmanageable, and set no bounds to their conduct, every display of an orange coloured emblem producing an immediate fight. For a few minutes there would be a lull, and then the spectator would see a sudden sprouting of hands and sticks above the level surface of the heads, a short sharp conflict, while the non-combatants surged away in a hurrying wave towards the footwalk, and a succession of battered hats, bonnets, parasols, and wardrobe debris of every kind thrown up into the air as spoi[ls] captured from the victims. As every tram came past, it was jealously scrutinised, and men jumping on the footboards did not hesitate to tear the orange favours and ribbons from the ladies' dresses, as well as from the men's coats. These depredations were seldom accomplished without an exchange of blows among the men, while the ladies kept up an accompaniment of alarmed shrieks.

Most of the fighting was done in the large open space appointed for the mass meeting, and one instance out of many will illustrate the kind of way that each spasmodic struggle arose and terminated. A buggy containing an old man and an old woman was wedged in the centre of the throng, and the old lady, who was rapturously watching the progress of a distant scuffle, drew a large orange-coloured handkerchief from the front of her dress, and waved it contemptuously in the faces of the foe. Three men jumped on the buggy like wolves, and in a second the old lady's bonnet and handkerchief, not to mention a few wisps of her grey hair, were down on the ground, and a lively battle was waged around them.

The captor of the handkerchief was knocked down by an Orangeman, who was felled with a blow from a stick by a burly person who had nailed his colours to the mast, so to speak, by stitching his piece of green ribbon into his coat. In less than a minute the fight was raging fifty yards away, and the ancient maxim, "Wherever you see a head hit it," came into existence with the automatic simplicity of a natural law. Many persons who had been lured into gathering armfuls of early wattle had cause to regret their devotion to the Australian national bloom, for the golden wattle blossoms produced unpleasant associations in the minds of the wearers of the green, and there were blows and curses in plenty. In political botany the wattle and blackthorn cannot grow side by side.

On all sides there were cut heads and bleeding faces,

but as long as sticks and stones were the only weapons used the damage seemed to be comparatively unimportant. A cry, however, arose that someone was armed with a knife, and a scene of intense excitement ensued, several voices crying out, "Lynch him, lynch him." The crowd made a rush, and a young man named James Holland, who had been making himself especially conspicuous, was arrested by the police and dragged into a cab. It looked long odds against the cab ever getting to the watchhouse, but the police formed up round it so determinedly that the attempted rescue was abandoned, and the prisoner was duly lodged in the cells on a charge of riotous behaviour, where he was afterwards joined by Jeremiah Slattery and Samuel Doyle, who will have to answer to a similar charge.

A pleasing feature amid the general disturbance was the behaviour of the Rev. Father Luby, the popular parish priest of Brunswick, who endeavoured with all the force of his eloquence to dissuade his unruly flock from continuing the disturbance. Mounting the front of a cab Father Luby delivered an extempore address of great warmth and power, imploring his hearers, in the name of the Almighty, to disperse and go peacefully to their homes. A few of his listeners shamefacedly dropped the handy pieces of bluestone, with which the locality was well provided, and followed their priest out of the throng, but the greater number, sad to relate, only stiffened their necks and took a fresh grip on their blackthorns. Then surging down the street, they joined the vast crowd that was waiting outside the church to greet the Protestants when they came out.

It was here that Jeremiah Slattery, armed with a paling torn from a fence, led a forlorn hope against the party of police who were conveying young Holland to the lock-up. His attack on Sergeant Brown was carried out with considerable vigour, but reinforcements speedily arrived, and constable Perrett took the too eager politician prisoner. Far into the evening the police patrolled the streets, and impromptu fights went on in every right-of-way until night came down upon the combatants.

(The Argus, 20 July 1896)

THE FULL AND TRUE ACCOUNT OF THE BRUNSWICK BATTLE

Last Sunday our reporter visited the advertised scene of the battle at 2 p.m. the first tram from Brunswick was the signal for a few to congregate at the locality, as it was anticipated that the "Oloi Polloi" [presumably 'hoi polloi'] would come on the return tram... Numbers of men had gathered about the spot, and about 2.30 the trams with their human beings kept stopping between Park street and Brunswick road; detachments of men came east and west from these streets, and the Royal and Princess Parks also gave forth hundreds of men coming in two deep and stopping near the Sarah Sands Hotel. One trooper was seen on his chestnut horse, doing patrol duty, and Sergeants Percival and Oliver with the local police were in evidence, but the sun glistened on few police helmets.

The crowd increased on the east of the tram line and soon a "Hello here they come" sounded, and a tram car stopped, from off the dummy of which a man stepped out wearing a sash of orange and blue, with devices of crosses and crescents, filigree[e] and other devices. Had the wearer had a necklace of snakes he could not have created more consternation. A rush to him, and yells of "Take it off you Orange Dog" rent the air, and the wearer took off his friendly society's badge of office, and rolling it up placed it under his coat.

A drag then dashed passed [past] containing several men in orange and blue regalia, following this came a two seated buggy in which were four young men, all of whom had an orange blossom, and as is usual, they with other wearers of the blossom, had to undergo a quick trial of their orange faith. An "Hurroo" and a crowd of twenty men rushed across the tram track from east to west and surrounded the vehicle; one man seized the horse while others attacked the drivers with sticks howling and calling "Come out."

The men were so taken by surprise that although they defended themselves instinctively, they had no show to resist. The driver with his whip handle made an attempt and hit out as did the others, but between the beating of the horse and the upsetting of the buggy, they were soon outside and on to the road. At the time this attack was made, there was only one policeman on the west side of the road, his number being ---, and he smilingly turned north and walked away. The local police under Sergeants Percival and Oliver had their few men on the east side of the tram line, but the crowd had so hemmed in the buggy that they could not get to it until the crowd were fought through.

By this time, the buggy being overturned and the late occupants thrown about and beaten, a constable led off the horse and broken buggy into the park, and assisted one of the wounded, whose head was bleeding, away out of the crowd, which by this time quite filled the open space in front of the Sarah Sands, and were perched on the top of the hoardings, roofs and lampposts. In the middle of the street there was a large crowd of Irishmen who occupied the spot where had stood the buggy, and these were shouting and hurooing and waving sticks, blackthorns, &c., &c., and cheering. In many instances the men held both hands aloft over their heads and yelled, "Huroo for Ireland" this was the only discussion of "The Irish Question" barring the flying of blue stone and whacking of sticks on the four or five men there was a set on.

Still the crowd grew thicker, and there was no attempt by the police to manage them, they set no bounds to their conduct. Every display of an orange color produced an instantaneous fight, a shove and a curse. A woman with a child of eight years of age that she held in front of her, kept calling out, "Give it them the Orange Dogs."

A cab came slowly from the north followed by a tram at a snail's pace, as it reached the thickest part of the crowd, Inspector Gray came out from the space and called to his men "men keep the tram line clear?" "Aye, Aye, Sir," was the quick reply, as the few men attempted to push back the crowd; but it would have taken a dozen troopers at this point to open the space. There were many cut and contused heads, and shoving and hustling, a cry was shouted "He's got a knife" and a scene of intense excitement ensued, several voices crying out "Lynch him, lynch him." The police and crowd made a rush, and seized a man named Holland, who had been battling and shouting like a mad man for some time; he was dragged into a cab, and after resisting an attempt at rescue, he was taken off to gaol…

The [Wesleyan] Church was crowded for service, but as members came out at the termination of it, hoots, yells and groans greeted them and woman paled, while men bit their lips, and crushed their regalia and bibles in their hands, while they hurried along to secure a seat on the tram. They were not, however, safe there as the tram passed along between the crowd, the men jumped on the footboards, and did not hesitate to tear the orange favours, flowers and ribbons from ladies dresses as well as from the men's coats, these they throw aloft or passed along to their mates. One big fellow, with a pronounced display of green in his hat and his coat, should have remembered that his green as well as his stolen orange ribbon should have gone aloft in fair justice to the occasion.

At the Church Slattery attempted to rescue Holland, but Constable Perrett snapped him quick and there was no attempt to rescue him. The Mayor, Mr. Methven and Mr. Fleming, J.P., were present in front of the Church, but as a riot had been averted they did not read the riot act, but the escape of the locality being the wreckage, bloodshed and disgrace was and still is a wonder to thinking men.

The whole display shows conclusively that some of them are no better than our fathers, and that the legislature in Victoria must at once stop any display of ribbon men [f]or 50 miles within, at any rate, some [?] of a town or city. The St. Patrick Society, the Friendly Societies of all other bodies will require legislation to amend the [U]nlawful Processions Act to make such a scene in Victoria an impossibility. It will take a small thing now to celebrate the fifty year old Orange Riot of Melbourne where life was lost, and perhaps last Sunday's rowing will result in a life going.

The whole fault of the fiasco was the inability of the police to cope with the crowd, the light manner in which the Hon. Chief Secretary treated the question of the procession, and all who were present must admit that had it not been for the forbearance of the members of the Protestant Alliance Friendly Society with their friends from other suburbs, there would have been a scene enacted on the Sydney road that would with the Eureka Stockade episode have helped to make an unpleasant chapter in our future history. At St. Kilda there was no row and the Orangemen walked, and tomorrow they hold Divine service again.

(The Coburg Leader, 25 July 1896)

THE BRUNSWICK RESERVE
To The Editor, Sir,

This reserve is not the correct thing for cyclists, not on account of any fault of cycle clubs. The football clubs, or at any rate some of them, make it a practice to kick across the cycle track while cyclists are exercising on the track. Last Thursday week there were at least 50 young men and lads using the cycle track to kick on, while 30 cyclists were training for the carnival contests. Not satisfied with kicking across the track, they wait until a rider comes round and then kick two balls at the rider as he passes. There have been several accidents lately, among them I got a nasty fall and broke my machine and hurt my arm and head, and was greeted with the shout "here's another over," and a sympathetic laugh. Our sports, be they footballers or others, must, if they expect the public to assist them, at least give fair play to all clubs and not because a football club has a right to practise at times, to make the cycle track the football ground, when other portions are better suited for ball kicking. The Victory Club has spent and collected more money than any club, and cyclists should have their track to themselves, at least from 5 to 6 p.m. each day.

Yours etc.,
W. C. Bones, Victory Cycle Club.
(The Coburg Leader, 15 May 1897)

DISTURBANCE AT BRUNSWICK

As the result of a visit to Brunswick of the band of roughs known as the Freeman-street "push", two members of that intellectual confraternity named "Teddy" Tierney and Alfred Watson were presented at the Brunswick Police Court yesterday morning, before Messrs. Hall and Fleming, J.P.'s. on two charges, viz. using obscene language and wilfully damaging property.

The evidence disclosed the fact that on Wednesday evening four members of the "push" drove up to the Caledonian Hotel, in East Brunswick, and, after having some drinks, started to fight with each other. Mr. Charles Hill, the landlord, requested them to leave, but was answered by a volley of such foul language that, calling a man named Anderson to his assistance, he attempted to put them out.

As Anderson was jumping over the counter Tierney seized a heavy freestone match-holder, and hurled it at him. It missed Anderson, but in its flight broke three bottles of beer, smashed two windows and a door frame, and finally struck a girl named Louie Warwick in the leg, severely injuring her.

Anderson was set upon by the gang, and very roughly handled, his clothes being torn off his back. Seeing that he could not manage them alone, the landlord sent for the police, and Constables Mahoney and Lindsay, who came on the scene shortly after, succeeded in arresting the two accused. Neither of them had any excuse for their conduct, excepting that they were under the influence of drink.

The Bench fined each £5, with £1/11/6 costs, in default, a month's imprisonment, on the charge of obscene language, and 10/, with £1/5/ damages, or seven days' imprisonment, for the wilful damage.

(The Argus, 4 June 1897)

ST. ALBANS V. BRUNSWICK ALBERTS

This match was played on the ground of the former. After a very one-sided game, the Brunswickites gave up at

half-time. The scores then were:
>   St. Albans, 6 goals 10 behinds
>   Brunswick Alberts, nil.
>   *(North Melbourne Gazette, 30 July 1897)*

ROUGH AND TUMBLE AT BRUNSWICK: A GIRL IMPLICATED: AMUSING EVIDENCE

At the Brunswick Police Court yesterday, before Messrs. Crook, Fleming, Trenoweth, and Stranger, J.P.'s, some time was occupied in hearing a case of assault, preferred by a young man named James Piper against two other young people named Dominic O'Donnell and Margaret Smith, which afforded considerable amusement. Piper was represented by Mr. F. T. Hickford, and the defendants by Mr. McKean, jun.

The plaintiff stated that on the 11th inst., in the evening, he was near his home in Percy-street, when he was accosted by O'Donnell, who asked him what he had been saying about "Mag" (the defendant Smith). Plaintiff replied "nothing." Where upon O'Donnell hit him in the eye, and a fight took place, in the midst of which the girl ran out of her house, and kicked him about the body, at the same time advising O'Donnell to "kick ---- out of him."

Mr McKean – You are Jimmy, the battler, are you not?

Plaintiff – Well, they do call me that.

Mr McKean – Didn't you ask O'Donnell to meet you at Nathan's hall for a "fiver'?

Plaintiff – Yes, to have it out.

Mr McKean – Haven't you made appointments with the girl, and bought her pastry? (Laughter.)

Plaintiff – She made the appointments; but I never bought any pastry.

Mr McKean – But you are a married man, with seven children?

Plaintiff – Well, I know that. (Laughter.)

Piper further said that the girl used horrible language when she was kicking him.

Mr McKean – How did you know the girl was kicking you, when you were on the ground?

Plaintiff – Oh, I could tell by the feel. (Loud laughter.)

For the defence, both O'Donnell and the girl swore that they were talking together when Piper came up behind the former, and struck him on the head, and when he asked for an explanation, Piper said, "Come over to the paddock, and you'll get it." Both then adjourned to the paddock, and a rough and tumble ensued, in which the girl tried to separate them. She, on her own behalf, denied that she had ever made appointments with Piper; and, furthermore, announced that "it would serve him right if she told his wife."

A witness named Murray was called, and commenced by vaguely asking the Bench "if there was anything they would like to know."

The magistrates put a sudden stop to the proceedings by dismissing both cases.

(The Argus, 23 September 1897)

BRUNSWICK SUNDAY EVENING

To The Editor. Sir,

As the father of a large family I feel both disgusted and aggrieved at what I see on Sunday nights on Sydney-road, Brunswick, where all the good people are supposed to be at night prayers. Now I think I state facts when I say that on last Sunday night, when going to and from church, I saw not less than 100 young girls, or children, as I may call them (12 to 18 years old) parading this main street with little bits of small, beardless larrikins, and brats of boys of all sorts and shapes and sizes. I am sure I am at loss to know how respectable young men will, in the future, be able to respect a good young lady when this kind of thing is allowed in such a civilised place as Brunswick, and also such a noted place for religion. I know we have plenty of pretentious God-fearing people belonging the many church organisations whom I think ought to try and remedy this

sad state of affairs.
>I am, etc.,
>A DISGUSTED RESIDENT
>*(The Coburg Leader, 30 October 1897)*

A YOUNG LADY REMONSTRATES
>To The Editor. Sir,
>Will you kindly insert in your valuable paper my protest against the brats who infest Sydney-road on Sunday evening. I think it is a great shame that these insolent fellows are allowed to molest every young lady that passes to or from church. Those who go to church are called psalm singing crawlers. Respectable people cannot walk in peace along the street while this sort of thing is allowed to continue. Thinking themselves manly in their actions the impudent boys crowd the footpaths smoking, and spitting over people's clothes. They stand at every street corner, too, using obscene language, and I think it is a crying shame that such things are tolerated here. A raid on the insolent gangs by a few plain clothes police would perhaps put a stop to this Sabbath breaking, and to the insults which decent people are bound to suffer if they venture to walk down Sydney-road between the hours of half past six and ten on Sunday evenings.
>Thanking you in anticipation, and trusting that my resentment will direct some attention to the disgraceful practice. I am,
>Yours, etc.
>A RESPECTED YOUNG LADY.
>*(The Coburg Leader, 4 December 1897)*

SCENE IN THE BRUNSWICK COUNCIL

An inexplicable wrangle occurred at the ordinary meeting of the Brunswick Council last night, between the mayor and Councillor Fleming. Councillor Fleming was explaining a matter in connection with a claim for a rebate of interest by a ratepayer, when he suddenly turned to the mayor and remarked, "You have been going round making reports about me that you will have to pay for."

The Mayor (Councillor Balfe) – Kindly explain that remark.

Councillor Fleming – I'll do nothing of the sort. You sit down.

The Mayor – You have cast a reflection on me, and you withdraw it.

Councillor Fleming – I won't. You sit down.

The Mayor – You will withdraw, or sit down.

Councillor Fleming – You have been talking about mortgages.

The Mayor (angrily) – Sit down.

Councillor Fleming (loudly) – I won't sit down. I order you to sit down. (Laughter.)

The Mayor (loudly) – You shall sit down, sir.

Councillor Fleming – I'll withdraw; but you will hear of it yet.

The Mayor – You will withdraw. Well, you sit down.

Councillor Fleming – I've got mortgages, I know; and you will hear of them, too.

The Mayor – Sit down. How dare you say such things?

Councillor Fleming – Oh, well, I'll sit down; but –

The Mayor – Sit down!

Councillor Fleming was finally persuaded to withdraw his remarks, which he did with an evidently bad grace.

(The Argus, 8 February 1898)

TO THE BRUNSWICK LARRIKINS

To The Editor. Sir,

Through your widely circulated paper I am, with your very kind permission, going to make a few remarks about that class of humanity which inhabits Sydney road nightly, their special stations being at the intersections of Union, Albert and Victoria streets, the most notorious, however, are the Victoria street "push", who, I believe, go under the sobriquet of the "Pie-stallers." As a visitor to Brunswick three nights a week, I can safely say that no single person of either sex can, without being insulted, pass any of these three "pushes", especially the "Pie-stallers", who make a specialty of unprotected females.

These "prospective" youths look upon the half-hour 8.45 to 9.15 p.m. (the time the police parade), as a concession, and they do not fail to take advantage of it either. Mind, I do not for a moment blame the local police, who do all in their power to cope with this foul-smelling "riff-raff", which ought to be treated by the scavenger as ordinary refuse – the scavenger to be supplied with a forty-foot handlebroom, but I *do* blame our well-paid legislators for not giving a little more practical consideration to remarks such as those passed by that able and learned gentleman, Mr Justice Hood, when passing sentences in the criminal court yesterday, for I am sure, if his ideas were given effect to there would be less cause for complaint and more happiness for the rising generation.

Yours, truly,
J.E.G., Fitzroy
(The Coburg Leader, 2 April 1898)

HOUSEBREAKING AT EAST BRUNSWICK

A Chinese gardener, named Ah Coon, residing in a quiet locality called Kirkdale street, East Brunswick, has communicated a very startling story to the police, to the effect that shortly after four o'clock, a.m., on Saturday morning, while his fellow celestials were absent at market,

two young men, by forcing the lock off a front door, gained entrance to his premises, and finding him alone in bed, they attacked him in a brutal manner and inflicted painful injuries to his legs and body with a broken shovel handle; his yells, however, failed to attract attention, and the disturbance was followed up by pots and pans and other articles being thrown about, and after several windows were broken, and the intruders were confident they had silenced the aroused inmate, they decamped. Ah Coon is confident he can identify his assailants, and several young men have been taken to him for identification by the East Brunswick police, but without success.
(*The Coburg Leader, 30 April 1898*)

A LIVELY SCRIMMAGE AT BRUNSWICK

Constable Green, of Brunswick, was the chief figure in a lively scrimmage that occurred on Sydney-road, within fifty yards of the police station, in that district on Saturday night. Green was coming on duty about 9 o'clock, when he noticed a young man put his arm round the waist of a woman who was passing and swing her round.

The woman screamed, and Green came to the rescue, and attempted to arrest her assailant. But at that moment there came on the scene an exceedingly fierce-looking little man, who threw his hat into the crowd that, as usual, had assembled to see the fun. The newcomer, who had a large expanse of bald head, followed his hat, and exclaiming, "I'm with you, Mr ----- Green," hit the constable a terrific blow under the jaw. Green was staggered, but had sufficient presence of mind to draw his baton with his left hand (his right being engaged with his prisoner), and when the pugnacious little man came on again he received what he afterwards ruefully described as a "oner that knocked him kicking."

It certainly knocked him into the arms of Senior-Constable Daly, who was coming to the help of his comrade.

The force of the collision sent both the little man and the senior-constable to the dust in front of a tramcar and after a short scuffle the pugnacious civilian arose with three trophies of the "night out," viz. a broken head and a charge of inciting a prisoner to resist, and another of assaulting a constable.

His name was John Banton, aged 45, and he is described as a bootmaker. The first offender meanwhile wrenched himself free from Green and escaped, but after a sharp chase was recaptured and lodged with his mate in the watchhouse. He gave his name as George Andrews, aged 20, and was charged with offensive behaviour. Yesterday Andrews's father attended at the watchhouse, and pathetically requested the police to let him go into the cells and give his offspring a "jolly good lacing," a recreation that the watchhouse keeper was compelled to deny him.

(The Argus, 30 May 1898)

STEALING AT BRUNSWICK BATHS

At the Brunswick court on Wednesday, two brothers named Arches aged respectively 9 and 11, sons of a poor widow, were charged with wilfully damaging the local baths, which are owned by the Mechanics' Institute.

The evidence of Mr. Goding, the librarian, showed that on Tuesday afternoon the lads entered the baths and stripped off a quantity of leaden gas piping, which they rolled up in readiness to be carried away.

The mother stated that she could not control the lads' actions as she frequently left home to obtain work, and whilst absent they had got into this trouble.

The boys were sent to the Industrial schools, the mother to pay 3s. per week each for their support.

(The Coburg Leader, 18 June 1898)

A LIVELY POLICE SCUFFLE AT BRUNSWICK

The Sporting Club Hotel, Weston street, Brunswick, which has gained notoriety owing to the numerous disturbances that have taken place, and necessitated the hotel being placed under police surveillance, was the scene of a lively and desperate disturbance shortly after 11 o'clock on Sunday night. It appears Senior Constable Daly and Constable Lewis, who were actively engaged on Sunday trading duty, visited the above hotel, when they heard a quarrel inside the place. After applying for admittance, which they could not obtain, they decided to watch the premises; some time after, three brothers named John, Charles and William Robertson emerged from the premises in an intoxicated state, and commenced to indulge in offensive conduct.

On being approached by Constable Lewis, John Robertson, who is recognised as a most dangerous customer, he having a very bad record, at once turned upon Lewis, and used most disgusting and vile language. On Lewis attempting to arrest him a desperate scuffle ensued, which resulted in the constable being thrown several times to the ground. The plucky constable stuck to his foe, and when he overpowered him he was attacked by the brother Charles, who in company with his brother William had been kept under control by Senior Constable Daly.

The scene then became a most exciting one, during which both constables and their assailants experienced a warm time. Lewis received considerable ill treatment by being kicked in various portions of the body, while John Robertson had his head cut severely by being thrown on the road metal, and he lost a great quantity of blood.

Finally, John Robertson was overpowered by Constable Lewis, and William had to surrender to Senior Constable Daly, Charles decided to quit the fray when he observed the approach of Constable Simmons, who had been attracted to the scene. After the two prisoners had been securely locked up, Lewis and Daly returned to the hotel in search of Charles, and they were somewhat surprised to hear him relating the occurrence to the occupants.

On entering the premises, admission to which was delayed, they found him concealed in a bedroom, and immediately on being discovered he made his exit through an open window. He was pursued by Constable Lewis, and after a very exciting chase, during which several fences were scaled and a narrow escape of falling into a deep clayhole, a return in the direction of the hotel was made, and whilst Charles was attempting to jump through the window again, he was caught by the leg by Senior Constable Daly, but owing to him having grasped a fixture, it was impossible to pull him back without injuring him; Constable Lewis, however, jumped over the pair of them, and in doing so, fell heavily on a person lying in a bed underneath the window; the room being dark Lewis was beaten unmercifully by the occupants. Finally Charles was locked up.

(The Coburg Leader, 17 September 1898)

THE TIP AT EAST BRUNSWICK

The residents of East Brunswick must certainly endure a pleasant time, judging by the reports that are ventilated in the council chamber in connection with the sanitary condition of the rubbish tips in that locality. A few weeks ago the council received a numerously signed petition from the residents, complaining of the obnoxious stench arising from garbage that had been deposited in a quarry, and last Monday night, Cr. Stranks drew the council's attention to the abominable smell that was arising from their tip, situated between Glenlyon road and Lygon street, and in doing so, reported that a number of rate payers had complained to him of the nuisance, which was intensified by persons depositing decomposed fish and leaving it uncovered.

Cr. Fleming said, as the nuisance was existing at the council's own tip, he moved that the Inspector's attention be drawn to the matter with instructions to abate the nuisance at once. Cr. Balfe, in seconding this motion, said this particular tip had been the cause of continual complaints.

The council's officers have had their attention repeatedly drawn to the matter, and he could not understand why they neglected their duties. Any nuisance could be avoided by the garbage being properly covered, and considered if the whole of the unused clayholes were filled up, it would tend to improve the value of land. The mayor, Cr. Wales, said the whole of last summer the tip caused continuous annoyance to the surrounding inhabitants, owing to the obnoxious effluvia arising therefrom. The motion was carried.

(The Coburg Leader, 24 September 1898)

A COWARDLY ASSAULT AT EAST BRUNSWICK

Considerable interest was displayed at the Brunswick court on Wednesday, when the hearing of a charge of unlawfully and maliciously inflicting grievous bodily injury upon James Jeffers a railway employe[e], at Lygon street, Brunswick, on Sunday night, was preferred against three young men named Matthew Heeps, tram employee, David Henry Tobrady, laborer, and James Walsh, laborer. The three accused who pleaded not guilty, were defended by Mr. J. M. Shannon, whilst Sergeant Percival conducted the prosecution.

Dr. J.Miller testified to examining the complainant soon after the assault at his residence, 28 O'Connor street, when he found a large bruise over the right eye, a wound an inch long over the right temple, a wound over an inch long under the left ear, abrasions and cuts on the forehead, and the right eye much swollen and blackened, the whole of which with the exception of the black eye could have been caused by a blunt instrument similar to the stone which weighed about 15lb, the cuts on temple and head could not have been inflicted by a ring; they could have been inflicted by a scuffle on road metal but he would fancy they were caused by the stone produced.

James Jeffers, a powerfully built man of about 6ft., with his head swathed in bandages, stated that he was walking along Lygon street at about 8 p.m. on the 17th inst.

When near Victoria street he was accosted by a female. While he was speaking to her he received a blow from behind, and was knocked off the foot path. The woman called out, Mat, don't hit him. It is not Lewis. Witness then threatened to give the man in charge.

Another young man then appeared on the scene, and Jeffers turned to go to the East Brunswick police station. Heeps followed and caught him before they had gone far, and again struck him, and he then closed with Heeps, and the latter fell. Heeps then picked up some road metal and threw it at witness, who retaliated by threatening him with a brick. However he dropped the missile and knocked Heeps down with his fist.

After this witness proceeded along Lygon street, and two men emerged from a verandah. Heeps called out, "That's him! After him!" The three then gave chase. Somebody else called out, "Stone him, Danny!" and witness continued to run until he was overtaken by Walsh, who clung on to him until Tobrady came up. Both punched him until Heeps arrived, and all three joined in the melee. The three men pulled him on a vacant piece of land and threw him down. One of the trio endeavored to bite his ear while the others continued to punch him. Witness caught Heeps by the throat and tried to choke him, but both fell. Heeps got up and picked up a stone weighing about 15lb. with which he pounded the left side of witness's head.

In the meantime the other defendants were kicking him. Heeps then called to one of the other men to hold witness's hands, which were over his face at the time, and Tobrady pulled his hands from his face and Heeps kicked him. A woman called out, "don't kill him." The clothing produced, covered in blood, was that worn at the time of the assault. In cross-examination, the complainant said he was a married man with a family, and had never resided at Gippsland.

An altercation arose out of cross-examination by Mr. Shannon.

Mr. Crook, J P. contended as the case was tried on its merits, it would be dealt with by the evidence before them.

Complainant: I have never been arrested, and you have no right to infer such a thing. He did not accost the woman. He was returning home when she spoke to him, and he never asked her if she was waiting for her boy. He did not have a stand-up fight for about five minutes with Heeps. He showed the constable the stone with which he had been struck, and that produced was the one used by Heeps.

Mr. Shannon: Were you ever prosecuted for assaults on women.

Mr. Stranger (chairman) the bench have ruled that such questions are not admissible.

Mr. Shannon: The majority of the court think differently.

Mr. Stranger, J.P.: If the other justices permit such questions, I will leave the bench.

To Sergeant Percival: He had never been convicted of any offence...

The defence was that the whole affair was a fight between the prosecutor and Heeps, but that it was a mere case of common assault. It was stated that Heeps was well known in the district, and had merely intervened to prevent prosecutor taking liberties with a woman whom he had accosted. At the suggestion of the Bench, the charge was altered to one of common assault, and the defendants pleaded guilty to that charge. Heeps was fined £5, in default one month, with £2 10s costs, and he was allowed one week in which to pay; Tobrady 40s, in default fourteen days with 30s costs; Walsh 40s, in default 14 days with 30s costs.

(The Coburg Leader, 1 October 1898)

LARRIKINISM AT BRUNSWICK

A half-demented youth, who is well known in Brunswick, fell a victim to a band of roughs on Sydney-road on Saturday night. Shortly after 9 o'clock, at which hour the change of police patrol takes place, an onslaught was made by some half-dozen larrikins on the unfortunate imbecile, and after he had been belaboured for a few minutes in a most cowardly fashion he endeavoured to escape by crossing a vacant allotment of land; but this proved futile, and only provided a better opportunity for a renewal of the attack, the "push" by this time having increased to from 25 to 30.

At this stage of the melee several civilians intervened but apparently only with a view to rescuing the victim, and consequently none of his assailants were captured. Later in the evening the crowd again spotted their "pick" as he was described by one of them, and hostilities were again renewed, but the encounter this time was brief, owing to the approach of a constable, who, however, was too far off to effect an arrest.

(The Argus, 3 October 1898)

SANITATION AT BRUNSWICK

The Brunswick council on Monday night indulged in a lengthy debate owing to a recommendation from the health committee, that the stable and manure pit at the rear of Mr. J. Allison's property on Sydney road be removed.

Cr. Allard said the stable and pit was within 12ft. of the occupant's kitchen and 5ft. of the bathroom. From a health preserving standpoint it should be removed, as the stench arising from heated manure was contagious.

Cr. Cook objected to such monstrous conduct of the council, and said the owner of the property had been compelled, at a cost of £150, to make improvements, and because their instructions had been carried out and a portion of the house was brought close to the pit, they are now ordering the owner to destroy what they had ordered to be done. A[s] agent of the property he felt a bit annoyed at the council's action, and unless the council was prepared to compensate the owner he thought their whims and fancies would not be carried out.

Cr. Balfe considered it a waste of money to have the improvements effected at such a place, as there was not the slightest doubt a nuisance existed. The council should not however make distinctions, as he knew of several places equally as bad, and unless the council were going to treat all persons alike he would not support the recommendation. He advocated that the Health Officer and Inspector should make a thorough inspection of all dwellings in the town and report thereon.

Cr. Fleming considered the pit most dangerous to public health. The council were crying out about protecting the public health and condemned the garbage tips w[h]ere no houses were located, yet they wanted to support that a tip that would be covered with flies in hot weather be kept 4ft. from a man's door. The tip should be abolished, and if the owner sued for compensation he would find it mighty hard to get. He favored a full report being furnished by their officers.

An amendment that the matter be referred back to the health committee was carried.

(The Coburg Leader, 22 October 1898)

A DEAD INFANT

A somewhat daring piece of work by abandoning the dead body of an infant was perpetrated early on Monday morning on an allotment of land located within a quarter of a mile of the scene where the notorious baby farmer Mrs. Knorr, carried on her operations. It appears that shortly after 8 o'clock a little girl named Ettie Dickinson, residing at Albion street, was going a message when she observed a woman alight from a tram, which had arrived from the direction of Melbourne, at the intersection of Sydney Road and De Carle street, where she threw, what appeared to be a bundle of rags on the ground and walk leisurely away.

The child anxious to ascertain what the parcel contained proceeded to investigate, when she was horrified to observe a child's foot protruding.

Constable Simmons was quickly communicated with, and after examination, he found the parcel contained the body of a newly born female child, wrappe[d] in brown paper and tied with a strip of cloth. The body, which had no visible marks of violence, was removed to the Morgue by Constable Scholes, where an examination disclosed that the child was killed by strangulation. The local police are busily investigating the matter, but up to the present no arrest has been affected.

(The Coburg Leader, 11 March 1899)

CHRIST CHURCH, BRUNSWICK: DISTURBANCE ON SUNDAY NIGHT: CONFLICTING ACCOUNTS

In Brunswick the accounts of the disturbance which took place at Christ Church on Sunday night, when the Rev. J. Barley Sharp preached on "Romish Reformers," vary strikingly. Prominent members of the Orange lodge state that they attended the church that night, with large numbers of their followers and supporters, on account of an announcement made locally that the Rev. Mr. Sharp "intended to refer to the unfair methods of attacking the members of the Church of Rome, and unnecessarily bringing reputable citizens into contempt and disrepute."

They listened to Mr. Sharp's sermon in patience until towards the end, when he spoke of the superior way in which the Romanists educated their children. They felt deeply offended at his statement that the Orangemen, and Protestants generally, were bringing their children up to be "nothingarians," and they also objected to a statement, which they assert he made, that Orangemen were very bitter towards, and had great contempt for, the Catholics.

They, therefore, rose in a body and left the church. They state that out of a congregation of several hundred, fully 200 left when they left, and before Mr. Sharp had concluded his sermon. Of this number 40 or 50 were ladies, and some were members of the church itself. The majority of the members of the Orange lodge present were not members of the church.

It is denied by the officials of the lodge that any

signal was given for the members to leave. They felt that in his sermon Mr. Sharp was apologising for and defending the Roman Catholics, and they also resented as untrue a statement he made that certain books written by escaped nuns could not be obtained at any respectable bookseller's.

Reports were circulated in Brunswick yesterday that several prominent vestrymen of Christ Church and one member of the choir had resigned, but that was emphatically denied by Mr. Sharp and by the secretary of the church, Mr. V. A. Clark. Mr Sharp added that one vestryman, who was also an Orangeman, had called on him and expressed his sympathy with him at the occurrence of Sunday night.

Mr. Clark states that the whole disturbance was caused by the members of the Orange lodge, who, to the number of about 40, with four or five ladies, were the only ones to rise and go out. Not one member of the church itself went out before the service was concluded.

The passage in Mr. Sharp's sermon to which the objectors took special exception was as follows: "Nearer home still, while Protestants plume and pride themselves on the superiority of their principles and organisation, the Romanists have gone quietly and earnestly to work, and will, in the long run, if we do not change our tactics, circumvent us on this most important point of our faith. What I said to a body of Orangemen assembled in this church some months ago I will say deliberately now – that in the matter of the religious instruction of the young the Romanists are in advance of us. Through the indifference and insensibility of some, and differences and division among others, the Protestant party, which might sweep the board if they were only united, are, in their present condition, in but a secondary and indifferent state. I urge you by all that is sacred to give this matter your deep and solemn consideration. The Romanists have separated their children from ours; they are teaching them definitely and persistently the elements of their religious belief, so that when they grow up they will be able to give an answer for the hope that is in them; while, on the other hand, sad to say, we are blandly letting things proceed on most unsatisfactory lines, leaving the religious instruction of our children to the vague and indifferent teaching given through a couple of hours in the week in Sunday-schools, and the uncertain quantity dealt out at the parent's knee. By this we will be at a great disadvantage. The definite Roman creed, with sustained and persistent instruction, will in the end prove itself to be superior to our irregular and vague system of 'nothingarianism.' If we would succeed we must move off these lines, and combine on definite and aggressive principles..."

It was at the word "nothingarianism" that the first sign of dissent was shown. Mr. Sharp asserts that one Orangeman raised his hand as a signal, and that as that gentleman moved from his seat the others followed. It is also said that arrangements were made during the afternoon of Sunday for members of the Orange lodge to attend the service, and signify their disapproval of the preacher's remarks, and that it was not until almost the end of the sermon that an opportunity was found by them to express dissent at any of his sentiments. On the other hand, the Orangemen deny that there was any preconcerted arrangement at all to create a disturbance...

(The Argus, 30 May 1899)

A BRUNSWICK FACTORY: SHOWERS OF SOOT

A serious complaint regarding an alleged nuisance at the factory of Mr. A. Sturrock Jun. came before the Brunswick council on Monday night, when Mrs. Sampson, a ratepayer residing in Barkly street, wrote to the effect that the volumes of soot emitted from Mr. Sturrock's factory chimney showered down upon her own and neighboring dwellings penetrating indoors and everywhere and defiling the houses inside and out. She forwarded several pounds of soot which she declared had been swept down from the ceilings and walls of her house.

Complainant also stated that a nail factory had recently been added to Mr. Sturrock's establishment and the din of the machinery rendered it impossible for people to talk in the locality without locking themselves up indoors. She had spoken to Mr. Sturrock in vain and now she appealed to the council for protection against the alleged nuisance.

Cr. Balfe remarked that this was by no means the first complaint they had received regarding Mr. Sturrock's factory. It was high time the council stepped in for the protection of the ratepayers. Cr. Fleming said that the soot from the chimney in question was becoming an intolerable nuisance. The factory had been set up in the midst of a populous locality and it was outrageous that the ratepayers should have their dwellings inundated with foul discharges of any factory chimney.

Cr. Hennessy did not think they should do anything to harm a local industry. He moved as a preliminary step that the council pay a visit of inspection to Mr. Sturrock's factory so as to thoroughly acquaint themselves with the fact before taking action. Cr. Methven thought that this was a wise proposal and seconded the motion which was carried.

(The Coburg Leader, 1 July 1899)

ATTEMPT AT SUICIDE

Mrs. Lucy Waddington a married woman residing at Victoria street West Brunswick, was charged with having on Tuesday week last attempted to commit suicide by drinking a quantity of arsenic.

Mr. Shannon who appeared for the accused asked the bench to deal [leniently] with his client, as she expressed contrition for her act and promised she would not attempt anything of the kind again.

Her husband undertook to keep a strict watch over her in future, and the accused, who seemed to feel her position very keenly, was discharged by the bench.

(The Coburg Leader, 30 September 1899)

BRUNSWICK POLICE COURT: "BOUND OVER"

William Edwards, residing in Nicholson-street, East Brunswick, applied to the Bench through Mr. Shannon, his solicitor, to have Frank Donohue bound over to keep the peace towards him.

William Edwards being sworn, deposed in answer to Mr. Shannon that he only spoke to defendant once before the 13th inst. He lived opposite to him. On that date his and Donohue's children had a quarrel, and defendant came over to his shop that evening and addressing complainant's wife said he would screw her b----y neck the next time he caught her outside. Addressing himself to witness, he said, "as for you, come outside and I will punch the b----y head off you."

Witness ordered him out and shut the door. Defendant then burst it open, breaking the lock. Witness was afraid he would do him an injury as he threatened the first time he caught one of his children out "he would do for it."

To Defendant: You did not go out of the shop when I ordered you out.

Defendant: Did I not ask you to come out that I wanted to speak to you?

Witness: No! You told me you would punch me if you got me out.

Mrs. Edwards, wife of the last witness, in answer to Mr. Shannon, remembered the date when defendant came into the shop and threatened to screw her b----y neck. She never gave him any provocation nor spoke to him in her life. He said he would do for her husband when he got him out and that he would do the same for the children. He burst the door open when it was shut.

Mary Ann Edwards daughter of complainant corroborated the above evidence.

Frank Donohue being sworn, said he never burst the door open.

To Mr. Shannon: He never used the words complained of. He only threatened to pull the childrens ears when he got them out. He went to the shop to complain to Edwards about his children. He was in a "bit of a rage" at the time.

Mrs. Donohue, mother of the defendant, was called and said she was in the shop at the time complained of. Complainants little girl was not there at all; complainants children were always biting her children who were very delicate.

To Mr. Shannon: She could hear what was said in the shop. She was on the threshold of the door. Her son never went inside the shop.

Mr. Crook, (Chairman): Why, he said himself he went into the shop and the other man ordered him out?

To Mr. Shannon: Was Medoway there and if he swore he took hold of your son and brought him out would that be true.

No answer.

Stephen Medoway stated that he lived at East Brunswick, and that on the date mentioned, defendant went to complainants shop to ask about a quarrel that had previously taken place with the children, and that complainant ordered defendant out of the shop.

To Mr. Shannon: I went over as a peace maker. I did not catch hold of defendant and pull him away from the door. I put my hand on his arm that was all, I never attempted to pull him away, I put my hand on him to bring him away, I was afraid he might get hurt. (Laughter.)

After a short consultation by the bench the defendant was bound over to keep the peace towards Edwards, himself in one surety of £10 and another in a like amount. 10/6 costs were allowed.

(The Coburg Leader, 25 November 1899)

ACKNOWLEDGMENTS

Thanks to the National Library of Australia –
a Trove indeed.

Thanks also to my three favourite Brunswick citizens:
Zac Winkler, Joe Winkler and Karen Ferguson.

www.ingramcontent.com/pod-product-compliance
Ingram Content Group UK Ltd.
Pitfield, Milton Keynes, MK11 3LW, UK
UKHW041303180426
11947UKWH00009B/650